WHAT I WISH
MY MOM WOULD
HAVE TOLD ME

May God answer all your questions

Dawn Mase

WHAT I WISH MY MOM WOULD HAVE TOLD ME

Purity 101

DAWN MAGEE

WINTERS
PUBLISHING GROUP

Published by Winters Publishing
2448 E. 81st St.
Suite #4802
Tulsa, OK 74137

Book Design Copyright 2013 by Winters Publishing. All rights reserved.
Cover design by Rodrigo Adolfo
Interior design by Joana Quilantang

Published in the United States of America

ISBN: 978-1-62746-313-3
1. Religion / Christian Life / Women's Issues
2. Religion / Christian Life / Love & Marriage
14.04.14

Dedication

To all the beautiful young ladies and their moms who have attended The Right to Wear Right weekends and all those who will attend in the future, you have changed my life.

Acknowledgments

This devotional wouldn't have been possible without the following people:

First, our amazing Lord, who put a simpleton's (my) hand to pen to share his message.

My husband, without whom this would not be possible. Not only did he give me his love, support, and patience, but his theological knowledge added so much!

My amazing granddaughter for her inspiration, and for her mom who spent her free time editing and formatting all content.

Laura, the daughter of my heart, who has journeyed every step with me from the first day of The Right to Wear White to writing this devotional.

Our awesome sons, Cory and Ian, for their support and prayer.

Trish, who started my journey to purity.

My parents, who taught me things in their own ways.

Contents

Introduction

This devotional has been designed for women of all ages who are in search of their purity. It is a tool to help them achieve that quest. Although the questions indicate moms and daughters (remember, moms and daughters of any age—it is never too late to communicate), you can read this with a friend or by yourself. Spend about twenty minutes together or alone, focusing on a topic, discussing it, making an agreement, and then praying.

Moms, I have one suggestion I have learned from spending many evenings with my granddaughter. The best time for you to get kids to talk to you is before bed. They don't want to go to sleep and end their day. Give it a try. Take time with your daughter(s), and you will see what I mean.

> Create in me a pure heart, O God, and renew a steadfast spirit within me.
>
> Psalms 51:10 (NIV)

My prayer is that God will speak to you while you share this devotional together.

—Dawn Magee

You, Not Anyone Else, Is Going to Make the Final Decision!

> But if serving the LORD seems undesirable to you,
> then choose for yourselves this day whom you will
> serve, whether the gods your forefathers served
> beyond the River, or the gods of the Amorites, in
> whose land you are living. But as for me and my
> household, we will serve the LORD.
>
> Joshua 24:15 (NIV)

My first question for you daughters is: "Why are you reading this devotional?" I'll bet I can tell you why—your mom said you had to. I'm going to ask you to take control of this devotional for yourself and decide that you're going to read it because you want to.

Why am I asking you this? Well, at our retreats, 90 percent of the girls that come, come kicking and screaming, saying they do not want to go. By the end of the weekend, 95 percent of the girls indicate that they had a great time and many of them want to come back.

Let me tell you why: because we have fun! We show them love, we do not judge them, and they learn something that is valuable for their life. You may be coming to this devotional because your mom says you have to, but it is my desire that you will come out of it with a greater self-worth and a desire for more wisdom; just like the girls at our retreat.

You must realize that as you come of age, someone or something (a group or philosophy) is going to try to set a standard of purity for you (or lack thereof). A standard does not mean a straightjacket. A standard is a set of moral and social guidelines that you set for yourself, yes, yourself. You will have valuable input from your family and friends, but they cannot make you do anything. It is up to you what input you let shape you. I pray for God to guide and direct you, for that is where it all starts.

Thank you for taking your time to get to know my heart through this book. My heart is to see you live the amazing life God has in store for you. Go to your Bible and look up Jeremiah 29:11. That is for you. See you tomorrow!

Talk Time

 Mother's Question: What was one of the hardest decisions you've had to make? Is there something you would have done differently? What do you feel was a good decision that you made?

 Daughter's Question: What is an area in which you struggle to make decisions (it could be what friends will think or perhaps just not knowing what to do)?

The agreement portion of each day is an accountability statement and is to be taken seriously. Once you sign it you both have agreed to follow through with whatever action is indicated.

Agreement: Write down the things you agree to do to help each other. Yes, Mom, if you want your daughter to come to you when she needs an outside view of a situation, then you need to trust her to speak into your life as well.

Prayer: Dear Heavenly Father, we know that the best place to go for input on our decisions is to you. Help us always to seek you first before we look anywhere else.

Mom: Thank you, Lord, for the mind you have created in my daughter. Help me to respect and trust her.

Daughter: Thank you, Lord, for my mom. Help me always to remember that she has wisdom you have imparted to her, which is important for my future. Help me to listen and know she loves me and only wants the best for my life. Amen.

Notes

What Is Purity?

The Spirit himself testifies with our spirit that we are God's children.

Romans 8:16–17 (NIV)

For the next little while, we are going to look at what purity means. How about we start with the dictionary definition: freedom from guilt or the defilement of sin; innocence; chastity; as, purity of heart or of life (www.definition.net). Now I'm going to say that that is a little over my head. Maybe I can help with some of my personal thoughts on purity.

Your purity does not go away after you are married and have a physical relationship with your husband. You will keep your purity all your life. Purity began at the day of your birth and is a gift. Purity comes in the form of mind, body, and spirit.

Before we go any further, I want to address the feelings some of you may be having; those that say you are not worthy to be pure, you have made mistakes. Purity is a choice, and it starts with a decision, that is deciding to ask God to wash you clean as snow. Right now, you only have to pray and ask Jesus to recreate that gift in you and help you to guard it from this day forward. As we say at our retreat, "Purity is a decision first, and then followed by actions."

You Are a Spirit

We are made pure (holy, which means set apart) from the inside out. What do you think is inside of us? Yeah, okay, you are right; our blood, water, and all our organs. But there is so much more. Let's start with our spirit. "Ah," you say, "Spirit. What is that?" Proverbs 20:27 says the spirit of a man is the candle of the Lord. Our spirit is where our faith, hope, and reverence exist and where our prayer and worship come from.

How do we keep our spirit pure? Spend your time on the things of God: prayer, worship and reading scripture. Believe me when I say everyone, even your mom and dad, need help in achieving this.

Purity is the inner intimacy with God's Holy Spirit Isaiah 1:18

Our spirit is sometimes also referred to as our heart. This is the part of us that communicates with God. This part of us was dead at birth because of the inherited sin from Adam and Eve. When we become born again (born again means asking Christ to come into our lives), our spirit is connected with the Holy Spirit and it becomes alive.

Before we are born again, we are ruled by either our body (physical desires) or by our soul (our intellect, our emotions, and our will). When we become born again, our spirit comes alive and communicates with God. This is our spirit man. God's desire for us is that we would be ruled by our spirit, by what we receive from God, rather than our body or our soul. Having our spirit man come into a place of dominance in our life is a process.

If this seems complicated, all you have to remember for now is that your spirit connects you to God so that you can talk to him. It is sort of like your cell phone to God; you can text or talk to him any time you want.

Talk Time

 Mother's Question: Tell your daughter about a time when you really needed to talk to God. How did you know when he answered? Did you follow his instructions?

 Daughter's Question: Okay... fill your mom in on the most important talk you have had with God and what his answer was. Did you follow his instructions?

Agreement: We (your signatures) _____ and _____ agree to spend time each day talking with God just as we would have a conversation with our best friend.

Prayer: Dear Heavenly Father, show us how to hear your small, still voice and be obedient to what you tell us. Even though it may be difficult to do, we will always put your will first. Amen.

Notes

_____

_____

_____

_____

_____

_____

_____

_____

_____

_____

_____

_____

_____

_____

_____

_____

_____

Purity of Your Spirit

But the fruit of the Spirit is love, joy, peace, patience, kindness, goodness, faithfulness, gentleness and self-control.

Galatians 5:22–23 (NIV)

The question now is, "How do we keep our spirits pure?" I believe the answer lies in what we feed our spirits. I can tell you from experience that feeding your spirit healthy things takes time, energy, and discipline, and it is not easy. Let's look at what your spiritual diet may consist of. Answer the following questions.

How much time did you spend this week on the following activities? (Yes, Mom, you have to answer, too).

- Reading: leisure, school or business-related
- Visiting with friends, either in person, on the phone or, yes, girls, by texting.
- Watching TV or movies
- Playing a sport
- Spending time with your family
- Visiting with God (prayer, reading the Bible or devotionals, worshiping in song or attending church)

If you were at all like me, "visiting with God time and family" need to be more of a priority. Over the years, I have worked very hard at spending more time with God and family. It isn't always easy, but the rewards are invaluable.

Through my time with him, I receive the fruits of the Spirit (found in the above passage). An example of this would be the difference in the way I now spend time with my granddaughter and the way I had spent time with my son.

In the first ten years of my son's life, I was not a Christian. There are many things from my past that I wish I could change, one of them being how I lived my life—which was not with joy, peace, and patience. See, when Cory was little, I was living in my flesh. I didn't produce the fruits of the Spirit. I worked very hard to make myself look so good on the outside. I believed that people would think I was a great mom if my son had nice clothes, a great place to live, and all the material things he desired.

In doing that, my focus wasn't on my son or God. By the way, God's desire is him first, then family; not work and other people. Providing all these things for my son and myself, I became overworked; my joy, peace, and patience did not exist.

Now that my desire is for my spirit to be right with God, I want to spend time with him and then my family. When I can do what it takes to achieve this I reap the benefits of this that I can't find anywhere else. I can see it most in the time I spend with my granddaughter. When she is with me, and it is just her, God and I, I am patient and joyful.

This is when I know my spirit is pure: when I see the fruits of the spirit present and at work. And believe me,

I don't always produce the fruits of the Spirit, but I have promised God that I will not give up.

Talk Time

Mother's Question: Share with your daughter why spending time with God and family is such a struggle for you as a mom. Or perhaps you do this well, why?

Daughter's Question: What is the area that takes up most of your time? Do you think maybe that needs to change or are you on the right path?

Agreement: We (your signatures) _____ and _____ agree to set times every day that are just for God, for ourselves, and for our family and to keep each other accountable through loving reminders.

Prayer: Dear Heavenly Father, we want to make you the most important part of our lives, followed by our families. Show us how, and forgive us when we don't make you or them a priority. Amen.

Notes

_____

_____

_____

_____

_____

_____

_____

_____

_____

_____

_____

_____

_____

_____

_____

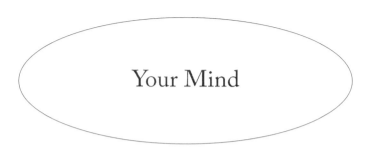

Your Mind

Your soul is typically described as being made up of the mind, will, and emotions.

> Don't copy the behaviour and customs of this world, but let God transform you into a new person by changing the way you think. Then you will learn to know God's will for you, which is good and pleasing and perfect.
>
> Romans 12:2 (NLT)

Let's look at your mind, which as we know it, comes in the form of your brain. Below, you will see a diagram of a brain.

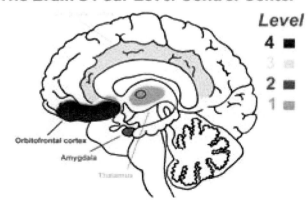

The Brain's Four Level Control Center

This information is taken from http://www.lifemodel. org/wordhtml/cc1.htm. This organization, through their study materials and conferences, has helped me to understand the brain in layman's terms. Let's take a look at some of their information on the right hemisphere of the brain. The right hemisphere holds an emotional regulation structure called the control center. This four-level control center tops the command hierarchy of every brain. Identity ("who I am") resides at the top (level four) of the control center in an area called the prefrontal cortex. Below who I am, the third level, or cingulate cortex, synchronizes our life rhythms. The lower two levels control our basic evaluations (level two) and our personal reality (level one).

Okay, so the above information does seem a little confusing, and it is. Even a brain surgeon would need to be God to completely understand the total design of our brain.

So let me just get to what we want to look at today: "If our brain were like the control center of a computer (the hard drive), do you think that what we put into our brains would be important?" Perhaps, you could think of it this way: I am typing this devotional into my computer, and when I'm finished, I'll save it, and once I hit the save button, the information I typed in is what is now in the memory. Let me ask you, "When I open it again, will it be different?" Right, the answer is, "no." Why? Because I am the imputer; I control the entries.

This is much like your brain; whatever you hear or see will be filed away into your brain as is. You may think, "I can't even remember what I did yesterday, so how can that be?" You are right; there are things we think we forget, but let me ask you this, if we just forget them, where do those thoughts go?

I can attest to things I thought I had forgotten as a child, they have come back to me, sometimes not in the form of a memory, but in an action or reaction I have. This makes me wonder if perhaps our thoughts only get buried, not erased.

If you choose to look at or listen to things that aren't appropriate, they too will become a part of your thought life. Is that what you want in your brain forever?

I remember when I was young; TV husbands and wives didn't even sleep in the same bed. Not because married couples didn't sleep together back then, but because it was not appropriate for the viewing audience. Now think of some of the things you see on TV (I won't describe it as I don't believe it is appropriate for any audience). We are becoming more and more tolerant of inappropriate material on all forms of media—even in our conversing with each other. As our tolerance increases, we sink further and further into allowing what is inappropriate into our minds.

Perhaps the question should always be, "Would what is going into my mind be pleasing to God?" I know that is where I want to be. I pray you do too.

Talk Time

Mother's Question: Tell your daughter what you struggle with in regard to what you have seen or heard in the past. Perhaps, there is something even today that you wish you hadn't heard or seen.

Daughter's Question: What do you think is the toughest thing you may need to give up: a TV show, some music you listen to? Take a minute and really listen to the lyrics of every song you like; you maybe suprised at what is being sung.

Agreement: We (your signatures) _____ and _____ agree to give up listening to and watching things that don't glorify God and keep each other accountable to our promise made here.

Prayer: Dear Heavenly Father, help us to guard our senses and only allow in what is pleasing to you. Amen.

Purity of Your Mind

> Instead, let the Spirit renew your thoughts and attitudes. Put on your new nature, created to be like God–truly righteous and holy.
>
> Ephesians 4:23–24 (NLT)

I believe the hardest part of our purity walk will be keeping our minds pure. Today, we are bombarded with so many different forms of media, all speaking impure messages.

Take a minute and look around you. If you're driving, there are billboards; my granddaughter very often points out a billboard and says, "Grandma that is inappropriate." There are inappropriate poses, girls wearing skirts way too short and tops showing way too much cleavage.

Every time you turn on the TV and flip through the channels, every time you open a magazine, there are those nasty pop-ups when you have your computer running, there seems to be no place sacred anymore. Inappropriate visuals are a part of this world, but remember, the Bible tells us, "We are to be in the world, not of the world."

The young men we mentor through our ministry are taught the principle of bouncing their eyes. I feel especially heartbroken for our young men. God created them more physical than emotional, so once they see these things, their minds go way further than they would ever want them to. That's why bouncing their eyes works; we tell them to immediately take their eyes off what they're looking at and focus on something that does not create impure thoughts. Girls, you can use this principle too, and you should. We are not exempt from impure thoughts just because we are women.

Moms, tell me, would you open your home and welcome someone in whom you knew would do harm to you and your family? The answer, of course, is, "no." Well, think for a minute. Have you done that? Have you allowed people to perform inappropriate acts or wear inappropriate clothing right in your living room on your TV set? Anyone can enter your home through your computer. I am not saying that TV and computers are bad. I used the computer for a lot of my research for this devotional, but type in *purity* and see what comes up. What I am saying is this: daughters and mothers, the old saying is "see no evil, hear no evil, and do no evil." A little harsh perhaps, but a pure mind is a wonderful gift. Steer clear of all that is impure; ask the question: would I look at, listen to, or read this if Christ was present?

Talk Time

 Mother's Question: What form of media do you find a struggle to stay away from? Perhaps it is something you watch on TV that you know is not pleasing to God.

 Daughter's Question: Well, perhaps it is time to 'fess up. Have you allowed something to get into your mind that affects you even today? Talk about it with your mom—she'll understand.

Agreement: We (your signatures) _____ and _____ know more of the truth now; of how important what we allow into our minds is. We will practice bouncing our eyes and will avoid impure images and sounds.

Prayer: Dear Heavenly Father, show us how to avoid or turn away from impure thoughts and information. Show us how we affect others in things we do which are impure. Amen.

Notes

_____

_____

_____

_____

_____

_____

_____

_____

_____

_____

_____

_____

_____

_____

_____

_____

Soul—Emotions

Like a city whose walls are broken down is a man
who lacks self-control.

Proverbs 25:28 (NIV)

All our lives, we will feel emotions. We will feel happy,
sad, mad, and sometimes just completely out of control.
God created us and he gave us emotions, so feeling these
things is all normal. As women, most of our lives will be
ruled by emotions. This is because God created woman
with a nurturer's spirit.

When you were a child, emotions were hard to
understand and even more difficult to express. I can still
remember when our young granddaughter at times would
have emotional outbursts over seemingly small incidents
such as spilling something. We found that after taking
the time to talk it through with her that her day had a
pile of things that had upset her, which helped to explain
her outburst.

In the change It takes time and maturity and sometimes a lifetime to understand the comprehensiveness
of our emotions. With the help of our granddaughter's
amazing mom, and as Madi grew older, she learned ways
to handle the small incidents during her day, so she could
better control her outbursts.

Part of growing up is learning that you have control over your emotions and in turn how you let them control your environment. Let me clarify, because none of us by ourselves can control our emotions, that we need the help of the Holy Spirit to accomplish this.

There is one emotion that seems to get to me most times and that is disappointment. Did you know that disappointment is created by feelings of surprise plus sadness? Because of my personality and my upbringing, these uncomfortable feelings of surprise come from a deep-seated belief I have, that things should be done when you say you will do them, no matter what the cost. Unless you're dead, you have to do what you have committed to. I also don't like anything unplanned, so surprises are not usually welcome. The sadness for me comes from my feelings that you and/or I have missed out on something special.

I need the Holy Spirit to temper this and other emotions I struggle with. If I don't rely on the Holy Spirit to change these emotions, my attempts will be futile and disappointment, like whenever someone comes late for dinner, will eat away at my relationships.

This is a work in progress, and every day, I need the Holy Spirit's help, as you will too. All it takes is to recognize we need some control, then to pray and ask God for help. Remember, God sends help in many ways; it could be a friend, a book, or maybe you need to see a counselor. Watch carefully for his answer, but remember this: "your emotions were a gift from God so they too are good."

Talk Time

Mother's Question: Tell your daughter about a time when you really blew it with an emotional outburst. How about a time when you blew it with your daughter? Talk about what would have been different if you had spent time with, say, a quick prayer and had asked for the help of the Holy Spirit.

Daughter's Question: Tell your mom what emotion is the hardest for you to deal with. For example: anger, envy, sadness or maybe fear. Talk about how you could work with your mom and the Holy Spirit to find a better way to handle this area of your emotions.

Agreement: We (your signatures) _____ and _____ agree to learn together how God wants us to use our emotions. We (your signatures) _____ and _____ agree to ask the Holy Spirit to guide us when we are feeling those emotions by taking time to say a quick prayer before reacting to situations.

Prayer: Dear Heavenly Father, show us how to use the emotions you have given us to glorify you. Thank you, Lord, for making us women and designing us to be guided by our emotions and intuitions. Amen.

Notes

_____

_____

_____

_____

_____

_____

_____

_____

_____

_____

_____

_____

_____

_____

_____

_____

_____

_____

Understanding Your Emotions

A person without self-control is like a city with broken-down walls.

Proverbs 25:28 (NLT)

I think this topic is best discussed if we dive into this area by looking at a few different stages of emotional development.

The following information was found on http://social.jrank.org/pages/228/Emotional-Development.html.

Around eighteen months of age, toddlers develop a more sophisticated sense of self that is marked by self-recognition and the emergence of self-conscious emotions: such as shame, pride and embarrassment. Michael Lewis developed a poignant method to study this development. A toddler is placed in front of a mirror and then the parent takes the child and wipes some rouge on the child's nose before moving the child back to the mirror. Although children under eighteen months are unlikely to show signs of embarrassment at the rouge on their nose, children between eighteen and twenty-four months do. Self-recognition makes possible a more sophisticated understanding of the self and brings about new levels of emotional development.

Adolescents experience rapid rates of growth and maturation of the reproductive organs and glands. Together, these physical changes accomplish the biological task of transforming a child into an adult. Rapid change, combined with a wide variation among individuals tends to make adolescents extremely sensitive to their appearance. At no other time in life are feelings about the self (self-esteem) so closely tied to feelings about the body (body image). These physical changes also affect a teen's social relations and emotions. That is why a pimple or, being ahead or behind a classmate in physical growth can be so stressful to a teen's emotions.

Probably enough facts, otherwise, it will just get confusing! Although this article concentrated more on the emotions tied to your daughter's physical appearances, there are still some take-homes here. I think one of the most important points in this information is the knowledge that your daughter is going through so many physical changes. Unlike that of when you reach menopause (I have reached menopause so I feel for these girls). Much like your emotions, hers are like riding a roller coaster really high, really fast, and then screaming all the way down.

Another emotional trigger is that moms of teenagers are usually headed into menopause, which means you now have two women whose hormones are changing and causing all kinds of emotional upheaval. This can be a guaranteed mix for trouble!

Try to remember that your daughter's outbursts and her trying to separate and be independent are not because you have done something wrong. Daughters, the same is true for you, not always are the struggles with emotions and hurt feeling because of something you have done wrong. If you can both see that love is a decision, not a feeling, and that every day you will need to decide to love each other, "then you will see God give you an amazing love for each other." It all starts by separating the action (emotional outbursts) from the person; you are both that wonderful, beautiful creation, God's masterpieces, just struggling to get a hold of your emotions.

Talk Time

Mother's Question: Tell your daughter which one of your emotions caused you to act in a way you regretted.

Daughter's Question: Tell your mom about a time when her actions in response to her emotions caused you to be hurt. (Mom, you are not allowed to become defensive.) Also, express a time where your actions to an emotion may have caused your mom pain.

Agreement: We (your signatures) _____ and _____ agree to count to ten before we express our emotions to each other or any other family members.

Prayer: Dear Heavenly Father, show us how to understand others and their feelings and keep actions caused by our emotions in check. Amen.

Notes

_____

_____

_____

_____

_____

_____

_____

_____

_____

_____

_____

_____

_____

_____

_____

_____

_____

Purity of Your Soul—Emotions

Be happy with those who are happy, and weep with those who weep.

Romans 12:15 (NLT)

Okay, I know: "How in heavens are we to keep our emotions pure?" When I spent some time in prayer asking God, what I heard is our emotions are a gift from him; they are pure until we use them for selfish purposes or we hurt others because of them.

So does that mean it is okay to be sad? Of course! But we can't expect those around us to be sad, too. They can empathize with us, but they can't feel what we feel inside, nor should we expect them to. What about joy? Does that mean those that are sad have to feel happy just because we are? No, but we do need to respect their space and not jump and bubble all over them. I have personally struggled with this for years. It is so hard for me to have someone sad in my presence; I have this overwhelming desire to make them happy and to fix them. So I can't tell you that change is easy.

What about anger? The Bible says in Proverbs 15:1: "A gentle answer turns away wrath, but a harsh word stirs up anger" (NIV). So anger is not wrong, but your words and your actions in your state of anger need to be controlled. What about people who are just plain mean or disengaged? Don't take it personally; most of the time, it's about what is going on in their lives, not you or their immediate situation.

My granddaughter is a gift from God; she tends to catch me in my areas of weakness. One morning before church, we went to get her breakfast through a McDonald's drive-through. The lady serving us was just plain rude and our order was wrong, and of course, I didn't handle it well. I let my emotions get the best of me. After we left, my four-year-old granddaughter said, "Grandma, we are Christians. That means she is our sister, you should be nicer to our family." As I have said, it is hard to always be in control of our reactions; however, we do need to take action after our reactions. We need to evaluate and may need to ask for forgiveness, and then, we always need to try to do better next time.

Talk Time

 Mother's Question: What kinds of things make you emotional? When do you feel the happiest? What things tend to make you sad?

 Daughter's Question: What kinds of things make you emotional? When do you feel the happiest? What things tend to make you sad?

Agreement: We (your signatures) _____ and _____ agree to help each other find healthy ways to deal with emotions. To give each other the grace we need when we have let our emotions get the best of us.

Prayer: Dear Heavenly Father, thank you for our emotions. Show us healthy ways to deal with them. Amen.

Your Will

No test or temptation that comes your way is beyond the course of what others have had to face. All you need to remember is that God will never let you down; he'll never let you be pushed past your limit; he'll always be there to help you come through it.

1 Corinthians 10:13 (MSG)

Willpower is inner strength, it is like a muscle. Take a minute and flex the muscle at the top of your arm, known as your bicep. Do you see how it gets larger and harder? When you have exercised that muscle, it will appear even harder and in turn, will make your arm stronger. The same is true with your willpower; the more you exercise it, the stronger it gets.

Why is willpower so important to the topic of purity? There will come a time in your life when setting good boundaries won't be enough. You will need self-discipline, which is created by a strong willpower. If you think saying no to someone else is hard, try saying no to yourself!

I have had trouble all my life with saying no to certain types of sweets. It's like someone else is in control of my brain, especially when it comes to me and a bowl of salt water taffy. I have no control!

Part of the problem is I wasn't raised in a home that showed me how to say no to things. As an adult, I have had to try to retrain my brain, and oh, it can be so hard! I am learning that for now I have trouble controlling myself when it comes to things like saltwater taffy, so until I can keep control, I do not have it around our home.

I am starting with things I can say no to more easily. Chocolate gives me headaches, so even though I really like it, I can only eat very little before I feel the consequences of my actions. These headaches provide me incentive to change.

Consequences are a good thing because they help us to see and feel a need to change. Consequences, I believe, are one of God's ways of getting our attention when we have done something wrong.

I have often thought that God watches even the small things we do, like me eating a full package of saltwater taffy. He gave me the will to eat it or not, but when I choose my way, he allows the consequences to take place. In this case, the consequences happen to be weight gain and tooth decay. At first, these consequences may not seem so bad, until my weight affects my health and our dentist bill goes through the roof.

God's heart is for us. He wants us to turn to him in times of making decisions and exercising our willpower. We are never completely alone, no matter how we feel. If we ask God to help us exercise our willpower and we do our part, at some point, saying no will become easier.

Talk Time

Mother's Question: Tell your daughter about an area where your willpower muscle is weak and discuss how she can help you to strengthen it.

Daughter's Question: Same as Mom: Tell your mom about an area where your willpower muscle is weak and discuss how she can help you to strengthen it.

Agreement: We (your signatures) _____ and _____ agree to help each other have a willpower workout every day. To ask the Holy Spirit to show us areas of weakness so we can strengthen our will. We agree to be transparent with our struggles and to ask God for his help and grace.

Prayer: Dear Heavenly Father, show us where we need to build our willpower muscle. Thank you for having given us each other so we do not have to work on this alone. Amen.

Notes

Purity and Your Willpower

When you obey my commandments, you remain
in my love, just as I obey my Father's commandments and remain in his love.

John 15:10 (NLT)

Willpower: do we have it under control or does it control
us? There are so many temptations, and today, they are
more "in our face" than ever before. Really, when we get
down to it, we are, in most cases, unfortunately letting the
world control our willpower, and we are not even aware
of it at times.

The Bible says to be in the world, not of the world.
That means we are required to live on this planet Earth
as humans until we are taken to our home with Jesus. Yes,
home. This life on Earth is only temporary, but our life
in heaven is forever. Can you think what forever would
be like? Girls, at this point in your life, it should be really
hard to do!

The Bible also says to store up our treasures in heaven.
I believe that this is where our willpower comes in. The
gift our God has given us is that of always having a
choice. No matter what is going on around you to make
you think you have to do something, *you* are the one who
makes the final choice.

Let's look at an example. Daughters, your mom or dad has once again asked you to clean your room. Everything inside you is saying, "*No way!*" but you are now in the place to make a choice. Your willpower kicks in and you agree to do it. Okay, we are not finished yet. Your willpower has made your mouth agree, but now, the true test comes in the action of cleaning your room. Well, now it's clean and you have obeyed. That feels pretty good, right! Maybe not so much because you did it, but you did it angry. If you cleaned your room happily, that would be where your heart and head had followed your willpower.

Let's say you chose to not clean your room; that wouldn't be using your willpower. See, being obedient or doing the right thing is using your willpower. You do not use your willpower when you disobey or do something bad; this has something to do with your sin nature (this sounds confusing, but I'll explain it tomorrow). We have a natural tendency toward doing things that are not being obedient or things where the consequence works against us. Think of Adam and Eve. They knew what was right, yet they ate the fruit. The struggle of willpower started way back then.

You will struggle the rest of your life with your willpower, but the more you do the right things, the easier it will be to do what is right. This brings your willpower into a state of acting in purity.

Talk Time

 Mother's Question: Tell your daughter about a consequence you had to live with when it came to not using your willpower.

 Daughter's Question: Talk to your mom about how hard it is to do things like cleaning your room. What types of things get in the way of your willpower?

Agreement: We (your signatures) _____ and _____ will recognize when we are struggling with our willpower and ask for help. We also agree to take the time to think about what our actions will bring for the future.

Prayer: Dear Heavenly Father, help us to forgive ourselves when we haven't quite measured up and our willpower has not been where we wanted it to be. Thank you for allowing your son to die on the cross so that when we mess up, we can always start anew. Amen.

Notes

Sinful Nature

> Those who are dominated by the sinful nature think about sinful things, but those who are controlled by the Holy Spirit think about things that please the Spirit. So letting your sinful nature control your mind leads to death. But letting the Spirit control your mind leads to life and peace.
>
> Romans 8:5–6 (NLT)

The sin nature is that part of the essence of the soul acquired at Adam's fall and subsequently passed on to every person at birth. The sin nature is the center of the soul's rebellion against God. The human soul has the following characteristics: self-consciousness: the ability to be self-aware, mentality: the ability to think, volition: the ability to decide, and emotion: the ability to feel.

Okay, I have tried to write this day three times. I know how important it is to share the sin nature with you; I just find it difficult to explain.

First and foremost, I want you to understand that everyone struggles with being sinful. We did not create it; it is in us from birth. "So who created it?" you ask. In his loving desire to have us love him freely, God had to give us the ability to choose. Unfortunately, Adam and Eve chose to listen to Satan rather than God, and their pure nature was corrupted. That corrupt nature has been passed down to all of us at birth.

God is so good. He knew we would want to be able to free ourselves from it. He sent Jesus to break the power of the sinful nature in our lives and gave us the Holy Spirit to enable us to live according to our new nature that was birthed in us when we accepted Jesus' death and sacrifice for us.

I thought I would give an example so you can perhaps understand the way sin nature works.

Think of it this way:

Daughters I am going to pick on you. You have done something you know is wrong. Let's say you went to a party that your parents told you not to go to. Now, you had been told it was wrong, you knew in your heart it was wrong, yet still, some strong force that you can't explain compelled you to go. When your parents ask, "Why did you disobey us?" You say, "I don't know." Well, I am here to tell you, it is your sin nature that persuaded you to go, and unless you work now on controlling it, it will get harder to control the older you get.

You will always have two voices speaking to you. You need to harness the ability to hear the still small voice of God and not the voice of your sin nature. So how do you do that? It starts with praying to accept the sacrifice Jesus made on your behalf and asking him to create a new nature inside you that wants to do what is right. Then ask Jesus to bring the Holy Spirit into your life. The Holy Spirit will be your check and guide, but you will have to hear and obey him. He is the small, still voice inside you. Jesus has made it so easy to have the Holy Spirit with us. All you have to do is pray this with me, "Jesus come into my life. I accept your sacrifice. Make me a new person and let your Spirit be my guide. Amen."

The hard part comes after, in working at having a constant relationship with Jesus, which allows you to hear the Holy Spirit. I don't mean hard as in he is hard to get to, I mean hard as in self-discipline. It requires your time and effort, praying, reading the Bible, and going to church. But once you have this relationship, your sin nature can be controlled.

Talk Time

 Mother's Question: Tell your daughter what sin you struggle with. Remember, sins are not always big. Even the sin of overeating is gluttony. Then pray and ask for release.

 Daughter's Question: Same as Mom: Tell your mom what sin you struggle with. Remember, sins are not always big. Even the sin of overeating is gluttony. Then pray and ask for release.

Agreement: We (your signatures) _____ and _____ agree that our sinful nature is powerful. We will seek the Holy Spirit to help us to overcome in the areas where we struggle.

Prayer: Dear Heavenly Father, help us to always repent of our sins and look to the cross where Jesus gave his life to give us life. Amen.

Notes

_____
_____
_____
_____
_____
_____
_____
_____
_____
_____
_____
_____
_____
_____
_____

Shame-Based Thinking

For we are God's masterpiece. He has created
us anew in Christ Jesus, so we can do the good
things he planned for us long ago.

Ephesians 2:10 (NLT)

Shame-based thinking is one of the most destructive
thought processes because it hits the innermost person.
It's okay to feel guilty about something. It just means that
you made a mistake and that you recognize it. Shame, on
the other hand, is when you start thinking that you are a
mistake and that there is something wrong with you. That
is where we tend to beat ourselves up and come down on
ourselves. We feel worthless, like we are less than others.
This is a lie, and it for sure does not come from God.
Shame drives you from God.

Some of the signals that tell us we are feeling shame
are when we are:

- Discounting our strengths and abilities
- Magnifying our flaws
- Judging ourselves by undefined ideals, such as other people's behaviour or unrealistic expectations
- Confusing what we do with who we are

Satan does all he can to keep us trapped in shame. By doing so, he keeps us from being as effective for God as we could be. His desire is to keep us feeling as distant from God as possible. He will remind us of our failures, cause us to stumble, and distract us from the truth of how God sees us.

Some of the other clues that may show us that we are living in the lie of shame-based thinking are: being defensive, liking to spend a lot of time by yourself, finding yourself in conflict and judging others, seeking power, being overly nice to people or blaming others, but most of all, if you feel bad about yourself, the root of that is likely shame.

Daughters, if you are having feelings of shame, find someone you can trust to talk to. Try your parents first. You may think, *No way, they will never understand.* But believe me, everyone has felt, or is feeling, shame. Talking it through will put it into perspective. If you really feel you can't talk to your parents, find a safe adult to talk to such as your youth pastor or a close relative.

Girls, please be very careful sharing these feelings with your friends. Friendships at your age are fragile; only because each of you is going through so many changes in your lives—emotionally, spiritually, and physically. The best thing is to go to God. Start by searching through his Word (the Bible). You will find that he thinks you are amazing, and if he thinks that, how can you or anyone else think differently? Also, take time in prayer, ask him to take away those terrible feelings of shame. I promise if you let him in, he will heal you of any shame-based feelings you may have.

Moms, remember, shame-based thinking doesn't go away with age. If you are struggling with this, please seek help and God is the first place to start.

Talk Time

 Mother's Question: Where have you felt shame? Are you over it, and how did you overcome it?

 Daughter's Question: What makes you feel ashamed? Do you have friends that confide in you about their shame? What are some of the things they speak of and how do you help them?

Agreement: We (your signatures) _____ and _____ agree to ask for help when we are experiencing feelings of shame, no matter how hard that might be.

Prayer: Dear Heavenly Father, you have told us not to be ashamed but to learn from our mistakes and move on, knowing that they are all covered by your death on the cross. Amen.

Notes

_____

_____

_____

_____

_____

_____

_____

_____

_____

_____

_____

_____

_____

_____

_____

The Wonder of Your Body

Do not you realize that your body is the temple
of the Holy Spirit, who lives in you and was given
to you by God? You do not belong to yourself, for
God bought you with a high price. So you must
honor God with your body.

1 Corinthians 6:19–20 (NLT)

Our bodies are designed by our Heavenly Father. When
you look at the body, it is so intricate that only a Creator
could have created it. Do you know that 50,000 of the
cells in your body will die and be replaced with new cells,
all while you have been reading this sentence! And in one
square inch of skin, there lies four yards of nerve fibers,
1,300 nerve cells, 100 sweat glands, three million cells,
and three yards of blood vessels. I could go on and on
about how amazing our bodies are, but I'll let you discover the rest on your own.

Daughters, this is a very important time of your life.
It is the rite of passage when you step from your childhood into being the woman God has created you to be. If
you haven't yet, you will very shortly experience changes
in your body. These changes are part of God's plan for
bringing you into womanhood, and believe me, it's a
wonderful place to be. Over the next few days, I am just

going to outline a few areas of changes you will see over the next few years.

Between the ages of ten and fourteen, most girls begin to notice changes taking place in their bodies. These changes, which occur over a number of years, and are generally referred to as puberty. The changes take place in all boys and girls, but they will start at different times and take place at different rates. Not everyone starts puberty between the ages of ten and fourteen, some people start younger and some much later. Similarly, in some people, all the changes take place in two years, and in others, they can take as long as four years. Generally, they start between ages seven and thirteen in girls and ages nine and fifteen in boys.

Puberty starts when extra amounts of chemicals, called hormones, start to be produced in the body. These hormones guide the changes that take place in the body. As well as causing physical changes, these hormones also cause emotional changes.

As a girl progresses through the stages of puberty, she will grow taller and her body shape will change. Her chest will appear less flat as her breasts begin to grow. The first sign that a girl's breasts are developing is when small bumps (sometimes called breast buds) become noticeable on her chest. Some girls find that their breasts or nipples start to tingle or itch while they grow. These feelings stop when the breasts stop growing.

Breasts grow into a variety of shapes and sizes, and many girls' breasts remain small throughout their adult lives. It is also normal for one breast to grow faster than the other. However, most girls' breasts will always be slightly uneven in shape and size.

Start of Your Menstrual Cycle

When a girl has her period, a small amount of bleeding takes place from her vagina. The vagina is a small opening that girls have between their legs. The bleeding will last for a few days and usually happens every month. This bleeding is referred to as menstruation and is not something to be scared of.

Most girls will have their first period between the ages of eleven and fourteen. Some girls will start as early as eight, while others may be as late as seventeen. Some girls get a white stain on their underwear before they have their first period, and this means that they may start getting their period soon. But it is difficult to know when a girl's first period will happen because everyone is different. This causes anxiety for a lot of girls, especially if their first period comes at a different time from their friends'.

When a girl has her period, she may notice changes in her body and mood. PMS (premenstrual syndrome) is a term sometimes used to describe the physical and emotional symptoms a girl might experience just before and during her period. For example, her breasts may feel sore or become larger, or she may get spots (pimples) on her face. She may feel tired and find it hard to concentrate, get food cravings, or feel very emotional. But no one can tell if a girl has her period just by looking at her.

With all that factual information I would just like to add that I believe the time of coming into womanhood should be celebrated. Much too often we make it a drudgery. Have either of you celebrated this milestone in your journey?

Talk Time

 Mother's Question: What was it like for you to go through puberty and to start your periods? Who did you have to talk with? What was your most embarrassing moment?

 Daughter's Question: What are your struggles and fears with regards to the changes your body is going through?

Agreement: We (your signatures) _____ and _____ agree to talk freely about the changes happening in each of our bodies and to celebrate the gift of becoming a woman (and, daughters, if your mom has not celebrated her time perhaps you can find a way to do that with her).

Prayer: Dear Heavenly Father, thank you for creating us as women and for allowing the changes in our bodies. Help us to celebrate the gift of being a woman. Amen.

What Changes Am I Going to Go through?

All the days ordained for me were written in your book before one of them came to be.

Psalms 139:16 (NIV)

When your body reaches a certain age, your brain releases a special hormone that starts the changes of puberty. It's called gonadotropin-releasing hormone or GnRH for short. When GnRH reaches the pituitary gland (a pea-shaped gland that sits just under the brain), this gland releases into the bloodstream two more puberty hormones: luteinizing hormone (LH for short) and follicle-stimulating hormone (FSH for short). Guys and girls have both of these hormones in their bodies. And depending on whether you're a guy or a girl, these hormones go to work on different parts of the body.

In girls, FSH and LH target the ovaries, which contain eggs that have been there since birth. The hormones stimulate the ovaries to begin producing another hormone called estrogen. Estrogen, along with FSH and LH, causes a girl's body to mature and prepares her for pregnancy.

So that is what's really happening during puberty—it's all these new chemicals moving around inside your body, turning you from a teen into an adult with adult levels of hormones (information taken from http://kidshealth.org/ teen/sexual_health/changing_body/puberty.html).

Okay, so that sounds oh-so-medical, doesn't it? Really, what is happening is that you are developing into a woman. I hate to tell you, but this change isn't going to be easy. Along with your body taking on the appearance of a woman, these hormones are going to play with your emotions and how you see yourself. This is a time that you will really need to confide in your mom; let her know how you are feeling. She has been there and understands what you are going through. And as a matter of fact, your mom may be going through hormonal changes herself, those which are referred to as menopause.

Mom, please never make your daughters feel like this is just old hat; that you made it through these changes and so will they. Try to remember this is a rite of passage your daughter is going through: from this carefree child to an emotional woman; help her through it gently and celebrate this time with her.

I don't know if this is true for you, but my mom didn't talk about or acknowledge the emotional changes I was going through. They were just ignored and most times thought of as bad behavior and treated as such. I can honestly say I wish someone would have walked me through this phase because I do remember at one time thinking I was going crazy.

I've heard a few stories of young girls that thought they were dying because of their periods starting. Moms, there is no need for this. Open conversations starting from the age of nine (studies have shown girls as young as nine start menstruating) will save your daughters from unnecessary worry and stress.

Understand where you both are and acknowledge the fact that it is not always easy to talk about how we are feeling and especially about the changes that are taking place as we mature. Open communication is a strong foundation for all great mother-daughter relationships.

Talk Time

 Mother's Question: Take the time now to talk about all those changes that are happening in your daughter—emotionally and physically.

 Daughter's Question: This is a safe time to ask your mom all the questions you have been dying to get answers to. I might add that your parents are the best place to get these answers, not your friends. Your parents have a vested interest in your future and you need their loving advice.

Agreement: We (your signatures) _____ and _____ agree to talk openly about these issues (that means, moms, sharing what you are going through as well).

Prayer: Dear Heavenly Father, thank you for creating these amazing, intricate bodies and minds. Show us how to prepare and go through the changes that are coming. Amen.

Notes

_____

_____

_____

_____

_____

_____

_____

_____

_____

_____

_____

_____

_____

_____

Your Beauty

Do not be concerned about the outward beauty of fancy hairstyles, expensive jewelry, or beautiful clothes. You should clothe yourselves instead with the beauty that comes from within, the unfading beauty of a gentle and quiet spirit, which is so precious to God.

1 Peter 3:3–4 (NLT)

At the R2WW (R2WW—whenever you see this, it refers to The Right to Wear White retreats) we begin the process of answering the age-old question: "what is beauty?" We take a look at what we think of ourselves, not just on the outside, but inside as well. Unfortunately, most of us concentrate on improving our outside appearance with hopes of creating an image of who we really are. Especially during our junior high years and perhaps somewhat into high school, we allow our physical appearance (our hair, our weight, what we wear) to drive how we feel about ourselves.

You know, the more I think about it, even back in biblical times, a woman's worth was somewhat tied up in her beauty (think of Queen Esther). Today's society continues to digress. Women have been made into objects through all forms of media. If perhaps you are questioning my opinion, let's take a look.

When I was attending college working on my marketing diploma, one of the first things we were taught was how all advertisements are altered from their normal state. The features of women models were always enhanced, supposedly to make them more attractive. If you get the opportunity, go to our Web site: http://risingoaksministries.com/, click into our resource area and take a look at the Dove video. It is a perfect example of how a marketing department digitally altered a fashion model.

The video shows in high-speed a model being made-up for a photo shoot. What is done to this model's features, and subsequently the photo itself, before being presented as a final product is astonishing. This is a prime example of how far media has gone to alter a person's image. In the meantime, if you see any advertisement, I can guarantee you every models picture has been digitally altered.

So for today, think on this: if media has gone this far to alter the features of women worldwide, who is setting the standard for beauty? Are you ready to take it back?

Talk Time

Mother's Question: Honestly, answer this question: Do you think you are beautiful?

Daughter's Question: Same question as Mom: Do you think you are beautiful?

Agreement: We (your signatures) _____ and _____ agree to honestly discuss times that we do not feel beautiful. To encourage each other to see the beauty God has created in us.

Prayer: Dear Heavenly Father, show us our true beauty, show us how you see us, and then show us what matters most. Amen.

Notes

Your Beauty Weigh-In

For you created my inmost being; you knit me
together in my mother's womb. I praise you
because I am fearfully and wonderfully made.

Psalms 139:13–14 (NIV)

We have discussed briefly that society, over the years,
has set the standard for beauty. Another example of this
is Twiggy. Okay, Twiggy may be a stretch; most of you
won't even know who she is. During my teen years, she
came on the scene as a model; she brought with her size
6 or less. Before that, one of the most popular stars of that
time was Marilyn Monroe. She was a size 12 to 14, and
most women were the same and comfortable with that.

What media doesn't express is that a size 6 is impossible for most of us. No one can have your body, nor can
you have anyone else's. You are built completely unique.
Your bone structure is different; your metabolism is completely different, even your blood type has been designed
for your own body to function. There is no standard
weight—just the perfect weight for you.

I have struggled with my weight all my life. I have tried
so many ways to lose weight! I have eaten for my blood
type, according to a metabolic test, Weight Watchers, and
so on. You name it, I have done it. I only came down to a
size 9 and still thought I was fat. I wish now I could take

back all the precious time and energy I put toward lowering my weight into enjoying the life God had given me.

I believe I would have never thought I was fat if people had not told me so. I allowed people to tell me what my body was to look like. We are going to talk about this more tomorrow, but in the meantime, I want you to take a good look in the mirror; tell me what you see. Okay, that would be hard as we cannot talk to each other (but I would like that), so write down what you see. Look at every aspect of your body and features, and yes, Mom, you too.

Keep your list handy for our conversation tomorrow.

Talk Time

 Mother's Question: Tell your daughter what it is about your body that you wish was different and perhaps who told you it wasn't perfect.

 Daughter's Question: Tell your mom what it is like at school and how people think they should look.

Agreement: We (your signatures) _____ and _____ agree to complement each other as often as we can to help boost each other's self-esteem.

Prayer: Dear Heavenly Father, show us your truth about our bodies and help us to believe in what you say, not man. Amen.

Your Beauty
Weigh-In–Part 2

> I thank you, High God–you are breathtaking!
> Body and soul, I am marvelously made! I wor-
> ship in adoration–what a creation! You know me
> inside and out, you know every bone in my body.
>
> Psalms 139:14–15 (MSG)

It is time to look at the list you wrote yesterday. This
may be difficult, but switch lists with each other and in
turn read them aloud. Was there anything either of you
said about your body or your features that was positive?
I don't mean, "My hips and arms are cute." I mean a part
of your body that you said something like, "I have long,
sculpted, gorgeous legs." Not many, hey. The problem is
that we don't see the beautiful creation that we are. And
that includes me.

God designed you perfectly. That means every part of
your body looks as it does because you are a masterpiece.
I know you are thinking, *He did not make me weigh what
I weigh*, and you are right in some regard, but he did give
you your metabolism and your blood type, which feeds
your weight. If you feel you are too thin or too heavy,
remember, if you are eating for health and strength and

not under—or overeating, then your weight is perfect for you.

What I would like to help you understand is that it is time to take your focus off your body. Please "know", that you are wonderfully and perfectly made, the create this word should have been creator of the universe created you, "God" focus on feeding your body to feel strong and healthy, and then accept the gift God has given you. Remember: you are beautiful; please don't let society tell you what perfect is.

Just a note* In most cases, when people say negative comments toward you or others they tend to have a problem with their own self-esteem. They mistakenly believe that bringing you down builds them up. You need to try not to accept their words and, even more importantly, pray for them. They need your prayers; usually more than most people.

Get ready to examine that beautiful face of yours tomorrow, as we focus in on our features and what ill-conceived notions we have about our beauty.

Talk Time

 Mother's Question: Review your list with your daughter and if you can, explain where those negative thoughts came from.

 Daughter's Question: Same task as Mom: Review your list with your mom and if you can, explain where those negative thoughts came from.

Agreement: We (your signatures) _____ and
_____ agree to accept our bodies and features
the way God made them. To see ourselves as he see us. To
work more on our inside beauty than outside.

Prayer: Dear Heavenly Father, we forgive those who have
said unkind things about our weight and we give them to
you and ask that you build their self-esteem. Amen.

Notes

_____

_____

_____

_____

_____

_____

_____

_____

_____

_____

_____

_____

_____

_____

_____

_____

The Beauty of Your Face

> Oh, my dear friend! You are so beautiful! And your eyes so beautiful–like doves!
>
> Songs of Solomon 1:15 (MSG)

I believe each of us wakes up on one or more mornings, looks in the mirror, and wishes the face staring back at us was different. There is always something we would like to change. And I find it amazing that as time goes on, the things I want to change are different, like the wrinkles around my eyes or my "not-so-lovely" arm flaps (I refer to them as bingo wings).

I can remember in elementary school, not sure what grade; we had a teacher whose nose was quite flat. I don't know where it came from, but I associated it with a pig's nose. I never said anything, but all the other kids did. Guess what? Well, what I saw was the similarities in this teacher's features and mine; plus I really liked her. Unbeknownst to me, I twisted what those kids were saying and my thoughts toward her, and I aimed them at myself. From then on, until I was an adult, I actually thought I had a nose like a pig. Until one day, when I had someone say to me, "You have such a cute nose." That compliment seemed to break a curse I carried with me for many years.

Watch that you do not equate your beauty with anyone else's features, either positive or negative. You are made uniquely perfect.

Can you imagine what God thinks when you look at someone and in your mind say, *I wish I looked like her?*

Think of it this way: your parents give you and your sister a gift at Christmas. Both are awesome gifts, and as you open them, you look at your parents and say, "I do not like what I have. I want what my sister has. I want it; I want it please, please." Your parents spent their money and time deciding on those gifts. They believed they were exactly perfect for you both. How do you think your parents would feel with your reactions?

Not unlike your Heavenly Father. He gave you your unique beauty. He doesn't want you coveting another person's looks.

Now take yesterday's list out and ask "God help me to see what you see about all these things I wrote down, especially the ones which are not so complimentary." He cries, "My child, I made you perfectly. I love how you look. You are so beautiful. Please do not let any human tell you that what I, God, gave you is not exactly what was perfectly planned for you. You are beautiful in every way."

Talk Time

 Mother's Question: Was there someone in your life you wish you could have looked like? Where do you find beauty in facial features?

 Daughter's Question: Which feature on your face do you think would look better if it looked like one of your friends'? Where do you find beauty in facial features?

Now that you have answered these questions, remember the Bible says we are not to covet, and that means not even wanting to look like someone else. "YOU ARE BEAUTIFUL AS YOU ARE!"

Agreement: We (your signatures) _____ and _____ agree to accept ourselves, to not envy anyone else's looks, and to work at loving our own features.

Prayer: Dear Heavenly Father, you say in your word not to covet. Help us to love the way you created everyone's features and to love our own just the way they are. I repent for the times that I didn't appreciate the gift of me as I am. Amen.

Notes

_____

_____

_____

_____

_____

_____

_____

_____

_____

_____

_____

_____

_____

_____

_____

_____

Purity of Your Body

> May your whole spirit and soul and body be kept
> blameless until our Lord Jesus Christ comes
> again. God will make this happen, for he who
> calls you is faithful.
>
> 1 Thessalonians 5:23–24 (NLT)

We always think that our body is the area we most need
to guard, but (as you have read in the days leading up to
this day and the days you will read that follow) the other
parts of our being are just as important, and in some
cases, even more so.

The issue with our bodies is that it is on the outside
and can be seen and touched by other humans; it is on the
front line, so to say. So how do we keep our bodies pure?
My goal is to provide lots of tips and tools throughout
my writings on purity, but the most important thing you
need to realize is that your body belongs to you and no
one else, it was created by God just for you.

Having visual images to help you when the time
comes to set boundaries for your body, I believe, will
make it easier. Let's start with what the Bible says: it says
our body is a temple. This word *temple*, in the Scriptures,
can be translated into palace. Every time I have heard
anything about a palace, there are always guards to protect the contents. So how do you protect your palace?

Ephesians 6:10–11 says to be strong in the Lord and in his mighty power. Put on the full armor of God so that you can take your stand against the devil's schemes.

Yes, you are in a battle. A battle for your purity! Here is what the Bible says our armor is: the belt of truth, the breastplate of righteousness, the sandals of peace, the shield of faith, the helmet of salvation, the sword of the Spirit, and the Word of God. You can read more about this for yourself in Ephesians 6. Each and every day, we need to put on the armor of God. Okay, I do not mean literally. You cannot wear the things above, you pray them on.

Another practical visual comes from a friend of mine. His fifteen-year-old daughter went from Canada to Scotland on a student exchange program. There she met a boy and began to date (remember, we believe dating age is up to your parents, and I am not sure this parent was in complete agreement with this relationship). When his daughter asked for his advice through e-mail (I cannot imagine being calm at this point), he replied, and among the things he told her was the bathing suit rule. The bathing suit rule is that *no one* is allowed to touch you where a bathing suit covers (and no, girls, I don't mean a bikini). If the time came when this young lady needed to have a way to share her boundaries without being uncomfortable, her dad had wisely provided it.

I am challenging you to make your lips sacred too. It can be done! We received a card from one of the young ladies that had been through our retreat; her card said, "Eighteen and never been kissed, praise the Lord, it can be done." I am not sure how you would tell a guy not to kiss you, but I think perhaps if you would say something like, "See these lips? They were made for kissing the man who will love me forever. If you are that man, on our wedding day, they are all yours."

Remember to set healthy boundaries for your body before compromising situations comes up; remember that Christ lives in you.

Talk Time

 Mother's Question: What mistake did you make in setting boundaries for your body? Do you know that purity comes the day you claim it? It is a decision. So if you have made a mistake, take your purity back today. All it takes is a simple prayer of asking God to return what the devil has stolen from you and from then on living a life of purity.

 Daughter's Question: Can you think of some creative ways to tell someone about the boundaries you have set for your body, along the lines of the bathing suit rule?

Agreement: We (your signatures) _____ and _____ agree to put on the armor of God every day and to help each other remember we are in a battle for our purity and that we are not alone.

Prayer: Dear Heavenly Father, thank you for being our protector and for giving us your armor. Help us to fight the good fight and remain pure all of our lives. Amen.

Notes

_____

_____

_____

_____

_____

_____

_____

_____

_____

_____

_____

_____

_____

_____

Self-Image vs. Self-Worth

> "Love the Lord your God with all your heart and with all your soul and with your entire mind and with all your strength. The second is this: Love your neighbour as yourself. There is no commandment greater than these."
>
> Mark 12: 30–31 (NIV)

A simple definition of a person's self-image is their answer to this question: "What do you believe people think about you?"

Self-esteem is how you feel about yourself.
Self-worth is what you are born with.

How do you feel about yourself: good or bad? Self-esteem may go up or down depending on what is happening to you. Get an A on a test and you feel great, but if you fail, you feel terrible. Self-esteem is changeable.

Self-worth differs from self-esteem. Self-worth is what you are born with. As one of God's creations, you are worthwhile and have value, which cannot be taken from you. You cannot lose it, but you can lose sight of it. You can forget your value.

Let's look at the Scripture we have above, "Love your neighbour as yourself." The Lord said there is no commandment greater than this.

Who do you love and value first? Is it your neighbour or yourself? Many of us were taught to focus on the neighbour and not on ourselves. As children, we are told not to brag or to be selfish. While teenagers, wanting to be accepted, we may have minimized our accomplishments to avoid appearing conceited. As adults, we may have developed a false humility to avoid looking prideful. We may even come to not like ourselves and believe that we do not deserve anything good. Your self-esteem suffers when your self-worth is forgotten.

The reality is that loving your neighbour as yourself begins by loving yourself. You must take care of yourself so that you can love and help your neighbour.

I was taught this in a course called *Choices* by Thelma Box, and now I use it to teach others why it is important to love yourself. I teach this concept using this object lesson: I give everyone three beans. I tell them this represents medicine, and this medicine is the only thing between life and death for your community. I have them form a circle (usually, there are ten to twelve people). I tell them that everyone in this circle needs your medicine. You are the only person who can meet with the supplier to get more medicine.

Then I tell them they have to look into the eyes of each person as they pass around the circle, handing out the beans (medicine). All they can say as they hand out the beans is, "I have medicine for you" or "I have no medicine for you." Those for whom there is medicine, get one of the three beans. By the time they have gone through the circle, they feel like they have let so many people down, and when I ask them if they saved any medicine for themselves, they never have. I say to them, you were the only ones who could get more medicine! So you needed to save some medicine for yourself.

This is true in life. If you have not loved or looked after yourself, how can you love or look after anyone else? Your love is like medicine for their soul, but you have to be healthy first.

Talk Time

 Mother's Question: In what areas do you not love or look after yourself?

 Daughter's Question: Same question, except I want you also to share with your mom where she could do better looking after herself.

Agreement: We (your signatures) _____ and _____ agree to help each other see where we need to look after ourselves.

Prayer: Dear Heavenly Father, in your word, you have told us to love ourselves. Please show us how to do that with humility. Show us areas we are neglecting and need to take better care of ourselves. Show us, Lord, how to help others to love themselves. Amen.

Notes

What Guys Think of Pure Women

> Treat older women as you would your mother, and treat younger women with all purity as you would your own sisters.
>
> 1 Timothy 5:2 (NLT)

At each retreat, we have young men, who are on the chastity challenge (staying pure until marriage), come and volunteer to serve our participants for the weekend. When these young men aren't serving, they are attending sessions of their own in respects to the challenges they face regarding their own about the challenges. They are learning the importance of their role in protecting and guarding the young women they are involved with, as well as the importance for them to save themselves for marriage.

One of the activities they are involved in is our Saturday night guys' panel. On Friday night, we gather questions from the girls attending. The girls are able to ask the guys whatever they want and the guys are asked to present their answers at the gala ball on Saturday night, in what we refer to as the "Guys' Panel."

Before Saturday night the young men are asked to read over each of the questions, they then pray over them and work as a team with our leaders to prepare answers. I am always so impressed and encouraged by the prayerful, thoughtful answers they give.

Below are the guys' answers to some of the questions (these answers are combined from a number of our retreats). *Get ready, girls, to hear something amazing!*

1. Why are guys attracted to girls who act impure and stupid?

   • Because those guys are impure and stupid!

   • Some guys see impure, stupid girls as easy targets.

2. What do you think about a girls purity?

   • It is very important for guys who want to stay pure.

   • When a guy wants a serious, long-term relationship, he looks for someone who is pure.

3. What do you think about impure girls?

   • Purity is where you are now, not what has happened in the past.

   • We want to avoid girls who choose to stay on the impure path.

4. How do guys feel about purity?

   • Purity is awesome, it's cool, and it's beautiful.

   • Those who haven't been raised with the right values don't value purity as highly.

- Even guys, who aren't pure, when they are ready to settle down, want to look for someone who is pure.

- If a girl has been sleeping around before marriage, it makes a guy wonder what they will do after marriage.

- The right kind of guy wants to save himself for a girl who will give her whole self to him.

Talk Time

 Mother's Question: When you were your daughter's age, what kinds of thoughts did you think guys had about girls about purity?

 Daughter's Question: What kinds of thoughts do you think the guys you know have about purity?

Agreement: We (your signatures) _____ and _____ agree to ask guys what they are thinking, not to assume that we know.

Prayer: Dear Heavenly Father, thank you for young men who want to wait for their wives. Please help them to remain faithful to that call. Please help the man you have chosen for me to wait for me. Amen.

Notes

_____

_____

_____

_____

_____

_____

_____

_____

_____

_____

_____

_____

_____

_____

_____

_____

It is not Fair to Compare

> When they measure themselves by themselves
> and compare themselves with themselves, they
> are not wise.
>
> 2 Corinthians 10:12 (NIV)

The Teen Esteem Council conducted a series of interviews to find out the major problems that teenage girls face today. Body image rated among one of the highest.

Where does this problem with body image stem from? Unfortunately, girls feel they have to compete to get attention from boys. And if that's not bad enough, girls are constantly comparing themselves to every girl they see.

Comparing is one of the most damaging things that teenage girls do to their self-esteem. While there are numerous ways girls do this, there are two that stand out. Comparing themselves to others and comparing themselves to the media's standard of perfection.

In group settings I use this object lesson to teach how comparing ourselves to others is a worthless endeavor. I hope it speaks to you. Let's say that I give you a handful of M&M's, and I say to you that you can eat all of them except the red ones and those you have to throw out. Now whenever I do this, I get asked, "But why?" I say, "Because the red ones are no good." The response always is "Yes, they are. They are the same as all the rest!" So I question, "Oh, really? Tell me why." I forever get the same response. "They are all chocolate covered with candy; the red is just a different colour." Can you see where I am going with this? We are all humans and created by God, each of us valuable, different on the outside but all God's children on the inside.

I promise you: after you get to know someone, the most important thing is who they are, not how they look.

Talk Time

 Mother's Question: Do you compare yourself to others (now share honestly, please, we all do it!)?

 Daughter's Question: Who in your class is the most popular, and do you compare yourself to her?

Agreement: We (your signatures) _____ and _____ agree to look to God for our value, not to other people.

Prayer: Dear Heavenly Father, show us how not to compare but to love people for who they truly are. Amen.

Not Judging Others

> Do not judge others, and you will not be judged.
> For you will be treated as you treat others. The
> standard you use in judging is the standard by
> which you will be judged.
>
> Matthew 7:1–2 (NLT)

While we are on this topic of not comparing, do you realize that in comparing ourselves to others, we are actually judging the other person? "Ah, yes," you may say. "But I am putting myself down and bringing them up." Really, any kind of thought about another person can be a form of judgment on them, especially when it creates jealousy. "Why do they have what I want?" Is that a loving thought? No.

Let's look at judgment a little further and see what damage can be done. I'll start by asking you this: Do you desire people to love you unconditionally? I would hazard a guess and say yes. Unconditional love to me means that you love the inner person (the heart), not the actions or the outward appearance.

Criticism, or as the Bible calls it, judging, comes in different forms. While it is true that some criticism is helpful—we call this kind of criticism constructive criticism (I like to call it feedback for growth)—most criticism is destructive. How does judging others destroy who

they are? Think of it this way: our words are very powerful, and we actually use our words to paint a picture of
who we are. Your words can also paint pictures of who
other people are. In painting these pictures you destroy
the ability for you and others to see people for whom
God has made them.

The two ways of criticizing are: face-to-face or behind
someone's back.

When you criticize a person face-to-face, everything
you say, negative or positive, will go directly to their heart.
Even if we think we can just brush off those harsh words,
those lies get deep into our hearts. These lies, unfortunately, tend to hit us when our confidence has slipped
or we are worn out. Those harsh words can continue to
plague and deceive us until such a time as there has been
inner spiritual healing.

So, let me ask you, do you want to affect someone's future negatively? I didn't think so. Nobody really
wants to hurt other people, and a lot of times, we do
it unknowingly.

What about those things we say about someone when
they are not present? I have personally experienced how
it affects the people you are talking about and especially
how they get treated. I still remember hearing from
someone about a lady who was supposedly always very
irritable. In my dealings with this lady, I would approach
her with my guard up and I wasn't very pleasant at first.
This lady wasn't irritable; she had just been through some
difficult times. As I spent time with her and got to know
her I found her to be a kind and loving person.

Remember, we paint a picture about someone with our
words, so look for the qualities that are good and paint
a masterpiece for each person. My grandma always said,

"If you have nothing nice to say about someone, don't say anything at all." I challenge you to take it further and find the positive in everyone and paint that masterpiece of who they are.

Remember this: the Bible says we will be judged as we judge others. So are the things you are saying about others what you want to be said about you?

Talk Time

 Mother's Question: Where have you judged and maybe need to repent (there may be something your daughter needs to hear)?

 Daughter's Question: Same as Mom: Where have you judged and maybe need to repent (there may be something your mom needs to hear)?

Agreement: We (your signatures) _____ and _____ agree to look at ourselves for what needs to improve and not to look at others as to what we think they need to improve.

Prayer: Dear Heavenly Father, show us how to not judge, how to be compassionate, and to leave the changes up to you. Amen.

Notes

_____

_____

_____

_____

_____

_____

_____

_____

_____

_____

_____

_____

_____

_____

_____

Positive Talk

And now, dear brothers and sisters, one final thing. Fix your thoughts on what is true, and honorable, and right, and pure, and lovely, and admirable. Think about things that are excellent and worthy of praise.

Philippians 4:8–9 (NLT)

Self-esteem will come from a place deep inside your soul. It is there that you believe God has created you perfectly and wonderfully and that he delights in you, his creation. However, before we can change our hearts, we first need to change our thoughts. It starts by talking to yourself the way you would talk to those you love. Think about it. Would you say to your best friend, "Man, you are ugly and fat!"? If you would not say this to a friend, why is it okay to say it to yourself? Jesus commanded us to love our God with all our heart and soul and love our neighbours as ourselves. Let me say this: If you think you can truly love someone and not love yourself first, God's word is clear: "It does not work."

We learn to love ourselves through the spoken word of others as well as believing God's word. First things first, I want both of you to take a piece of paper and I want you to list all the great qualities (make sure you also look at characteristics and virtues) the other person has. Moms for daughters, and then the other way around. Now read those words slowly and clearly to each other. I'll bet you didn't expect someone to think so highly of you. Do not lose that paper; put it on your mirror, and every time, you look in that mirror, read off that list. You could even add a few of your own thoughts about how wonderful you are. Remember, it is important to take the time to build each other's self-esteem. Find something every day that you can say to each other that is positive.

Just a thought, Moms: when I look back at raising my son, I was sure that I was to help him be a better person, and that is partially true. I want to be proud of him. We tend to see ourselves through our kids, and we think everyone else does as well. We find in them all the characteristics, shortcomings, and habits we don't like in ourselves. Then we go about trying to fix those. Relax. God is the one in charge of the repairs. Your job is to love, give patient instructions, and then let God change those things that need to be changed (and just a note— not all things need repair). Your most important job is to find the gifts and positive traits in your children and build them up. God's word tells us to lift people up, not tear them down. Girls, it might be wise to rethink how you talk to your parents, too. Are your words positive and encouraging?

Perhaps, if we could remember God is always with us and to ask him if he likes the things we say to ourselves or others.

Talk Time

Mother's Question: What are some of the areas you criticize yourself in? Why do you think you do that, and what do you think you can do to change that behaviour?

Daughter's Question: Same as Mom: What are some of the areas you criticize yourself in? Why do you think you do that, and what do you think you can do to change that behaviour?

Agreement: We (your signatures) _____ and _____ agree to be more loving toward ourselves and to accept each other for who we are. Together, we are building up each other's confidence!

Prayer: Dear Heavenly Father, when we struggle with who we are, show us what you think about us. Amen.

Notes

_____

_____

_____

_____

_____

_____

_____

_____

_____

_____

_____

_____

_____

_____

Power of Words

Everyone enjoys a fitting reply; it is wonderful to
say the right thing at the right time!

Proverbs 15:23 (NLT)

One of the simplest ways to change your self-talk is to
change what you say to yourself. God says that we carry
life and death in the power of our tongues. He not only
meant what we say to others, but what we say to ourselves.
How many times a day do you criticize yourself? We very
seldom take the time to listen to what we are saying to
ourselves; it just becomes habit. Make a mental note (or if
you are like me, write it down and place it where you can
see it) over the next few weeks, listen to the words you
speak to yourself and others. Then give some thought to
what needs to change.

There is a game we play whenever our granddaughter
comes for dinner. We start with highs (what was good
about your day), lows (what was rough), and then we
take time to compliment everyone individually. There are
times where it is difficult, especially when new people are
over, but when we are finished, it is always enjoyed. The
cutest part is when our granddaughter tells her grandparents not to get all lovey-dovey. Even though she says
that, you know what an impact it makes on her, when her
grandparents genuinely speak loving words to each other.

I challenge you over the next while to make this a part of your dinnertime, or at least spend time complimenting everyone close to you.

Not only does what we say to ourselves matter, but we need to hear uplifting words from others. When you find you are speaking negative words to yourself, the easiest way to change this is to focus on the words you speak. Listen to the words that you speak most often; for example, one of mine seems to be *stupid*. Whenever I catch myself, I say something like, "Stupid? Impossible! I'm brilliant." Now I don't go around publicly announcing I am brilliant; that would be prideful.

Below is a list of some common words we say to ourselves every day. Perhaps starting today you could work at changing your vocabulary and in turn changing your life.

Go ahead say them out loud, just see the difference.

PAIN WORDS	POWER WORDS
I can't	I won't
I should	I could
It's not my fault	I'm responsible for what I have done
It's a problem	It's an opportunity
I'm never satisfied	I want to learn and grow
Life's a struggle	Life's an adventure
I hope	I know
If only	Next time
What will I do?	I know I can handle it
It's terrible	It's a learning experience

Talk Time

Mother's Question: What are some words that you can alter to change how you feel about yourself?

Daughter's Question: What are some words that you can alter to change how you feel about yourself?

Agreement: We (your signatures) _____ and _____ agree to make more of an effort to change the words we speak to ourselves and each other—by speaking words that lift up, not tear down.

Prayer: Dear Heavenly Father, help us to speak to ourselves as you would—with love and compassion. Amen.

Notes

Finding the Unique Person Called You

> You saw me before I was born. Every day of my
> life was recorded in your book. Every moment
> was laid out before a single day had passed.
>
> Psalm 139:16 (NLT)

Have you ever asked, "Why am I me and why am I here?"

In my life, as well as in my career as a life and business coach, the two things that are always at the forefront of what people want to know (and girls, these are adults your mom and dad's age) is, "Why am I here on Earth and who am I really?" This is one of my favourite areas to work through with them. I get to help them seek their Creator and ask him what his plans were when he made them.

The more I study this area, the more I have come to believe our purpose on Earth starts right from the time of our birth.

Close your eyes for a minute and imagine our Heavenly Father designing you. He is knitting together all your body parts, features, your mind, and now, he is going to breathe life into you. I imagine, as he did in the creation of the Earth, he now speaks your purpose into your being. I do not have the answers to what your purpose is. Only you have those answers, and you will only find them by seeking (your creator) God and experiencing life. At this time and in the place where you are right now you have a purpose only you can fill.

Finding your purpose may seem like an overwhelming task; there are so many things to do, and God at times may seem so far away. I do believe, however, that God gives us clues; we just need to be in search of them. Over the next few days, we are going to have conversations that may help you see some of those clues for yourself and in turn, start the journey of discovering your purpose in life.

A good book for you to pick up on finding your purpose is *The Path* by Laurie Beth Jones. This book will lead you through practical exercises to help you discover what your life purpose is. I truly enjoyed this read, and at over fifty years of age, I found a new sense of purpose through this book.

Praying, reading, and asking people questions are like the clues on a treasure map. Finding your purpose is an adventure, just like searching for a treasure. I hope you have started that adventure today!

Talk Time

Mother's Question: Have you been able to find your purpose? If so, share it with your daughter. If not, discuss how not knowing your purpose has affected you.

Daughter's Question: Ask your mom, from the time of your birth until now, what she has seen as your strengths and talents.

Agreement: We (your signatures) _____ and _____ agree to seek together what God has created us to do in life and not to pressure each other into a purpose that is not ours.

Prayer: Dear Heavenly Father, show us the clues that will lead us to know what it is you have designed us to do. Amen.

Notes

> I know what I'm doing. I have it all planned out–
> plans to take care of you, not abandon you, plans
> to give you the future you hope for.
>
> Jeremiah 29:11 (msg)

God has shown me a picture for the search of our purpose. He showed it in the form of a treasure hunt. Have you ever been on a treasure hunt? It is so much easier if you have a map containing clues. That is how I now see our life purpose; as a treasure hunt. X marks the spot. I believe the X that marks the spot is found in Luke 4:43. "But he said, I must preach the good news of the kingdom of God to the other towns also, because that is why I was sent."

Don't worry. This does not mean that we were all born to preach from a pulpit. No, means that wherever we are, our job is to be a shining light in a world of darkness. Your main purpose on Earth is to worship our God and share the good news. Where you are called to do that will be part of what we discover as your purpose.

I believe there is a huge fear associated with sharing our faith (daughters, especially for your age group). The fear of, "I do not know enough about God," "I cannot memorize scripture," or "My friends will think I am a

Jesus freak." And you're right. All these things could happen. But I'll tell you this: all God asks is for us to be who we are, know what you know, and then just allow him to show us what to do. I can even promise you this: if you leave yourself open to his promptings, you will see amazing things for the kingdom of God occur.

I do not have a lot of Scripture memorized. I also do not have all the answers or confidence to help people who ask me to help them find the truth (Jesus). I also do not want to look foolish. I am no different than you, just older. God has always given me the words to say or closed the ears of people when I said something unneeded or not helpful. I have never had to do anything crazy, but I have had opportunities to minister to people just through how I act and who I am.

Tomorrow, we will look at some other areas of purpose such as callings, employment, and things like that. For today, know that your first and foremost purpose is to be a vessel for God to work through. Say to him every day, "As you wish, Lord!"

Talk Time

 Mother's Question: Have you experienced a time when God used you? Share what happened and how it made you feel.

 Daughter's Question: Same question as your mom, but add what your fears are of letting God use you.

Agreement: We (your signatures) _____ and _____ agree to allow God to work through us.

Prayer: Dear Heavenly Father, give us a passion to share your good news with everyone we meet. Help us to remember that you have a plan for our lives just as you say in your word, in Jeremiah 29:11. Amen.

Notes

_____

_____

_____

_____

_____

_____

_____

_____

_____

_____

_____

_____

_____

_____

_____

Finding Your Purpose/Calling Part 2

You can make many plans, but the Lord's purpose will prevail.

Proverbs 19:21 (NLT)

If you do not know where you are going, how are you ever going to get there? Let's take a look at where you may be headed.

If you can imagine walking in a dark forest and all you have with you is a flashlight to guide your steps, "what would you do?" Would you shine the flashlight over on the trees beside you or point it up to the sky? "No." In order to see where you are going, you keep it focused on the path. The flashlight will not show you ten feet ahead. If it did, you might not go there, it might be too frightening. Instead, the light shows you just far enough to get you safely to the next step.

Like the flashlight shining too far ahead, I believe with our purpose/calling that if God showed us today all he has in store for our future, we would not be ready. We may even be so afraid that we would run away. In God's word, he talks about living in today, not to worry about tomorrow. Although keep in mind that he also clearly talks about planning, he says, without it, people perish.

Our path can be altered through what life hands us, but our purpose never will be. Our path may get rocky or even too steep to climb, until we gain the strength it takes, but God is with us always.

Over the next few days I am going to ask you many questions. As we discussed earlier, your purpose is like a treasure hunt. The clues for your treasure hunt will be all the questions asked over the next few days; below are a few questions to get you started

What fills you with joy? This could be music, organizing, other people, being with kids... just think of the times you felt the happiest.

What makes you mad, and those feelings urge you on to make a difference and do something about it? This could be someone belittling you or those you care about, animals being hurt, kids with no food, or how something has been said...

Note: Make sure to keep your answers to all the above questions handy. We will use them at the end of our discussion on purpose and calling to help you design the first draft of your mission statement.

Talk Time

 Mother's Question: What talent does your daughter have that you see is leading her to her purpose?

 Daughter's Question: What talent does your mom have that you see is part of her purpose?

Agreement: We (your signatures) _____ and _____ agree to be on the lookout, to be alert for hints from God that may be telling us his purpose for our lives.

Prayer: Dear Heavenly Father, thank you for creating us with a greater calling than we could ever imagine. Help us to listen to your voice and to know we have a purpose here on Earth. Amen.

Notes

Finding Your Purpose/Calling Part 3

Before I formed you in the womb I knew you, before you were born I set you apart.

Jeremiah 1:5 (NIV)

Are you ready for another day of treasure hunting? Today, we will take the time to answer these questions (Yes, Mom, you too):

The following are some questions from the book, *The Path* by Laurie Beth Jones:

What did you do for fun when you were a child?

What were your favorite toys?

What did you tell people you were going to do or be when you grew up?

People say, "Oh, you are so good at_____."
Write down a list of no less than twenty talents you have been given. Pretend that you will be given a $1,000 bill for every talent you list.

Which of those talents have you buried (done nothing with)?

Which of those talents have you multiplied (used to the benefit of others or yourself)?

Note: Keep your notes from today handy as well.

Talk Time

 Mother's Question: What did you dream you would do or be? Are you living that now?

 Daughter's Question: What dreams do you have for your future?

Agreement: We (your signatures) _____ and _____ agree to help each follow our dreams (the desires of our heart that are put there by God).

Prayer: Dear Heavenly Father, thank you for giving us the desires of our heart—your desire. Help us to live that out. Amen.

Finding Your Purpose/Calling Part 4

I cry out to God Most High, to God who will fulfill his purpose for me.

Psalms 57:2 (NLT)

Below is another exercise I found in *The Path* by Laurie Beth Jones (there is so much more in this book, make sure to purchase it). This too will help us with that treasure hunt we are on, "finding your purpose."

Below is a list of verbs. Pick out the three verbs from each column that most excite you. Then, from that list of verbs, narrow it down and select the ultimate three (it is the verbs we choose to act on that shed light on who we are.)

Accomplishment / Success	Flair	Punctuality
Accountability	Freedom	Quality of work
Accuracy	Friendship	Regularity
Adventure	Fun	Reliability
Achievement	Global view	Resourcefulness
All for one and one for all	Good will	Respect for others
Beauty	Goodness	Responsiveness
Calm / quietude / peace	Gratitude	Results-oriented
Challenge	Hard work	Rule of law
Change	Harmony	Safety
Cleanliness / orderliness	Honesty	Satisfying others
Collaboration	Honor	Security
Commitment	Improvement	Self-giving
Communication	Independence	Self-thinking
Community	Individuality	Service (to others / society)
Competence	Inner peace / calm / quietude	Simplicity
Competition	Innovation	Skill
Concern for others	Integrity	Solving problems
Connection	Intensity	Sped
Content over form	Justice	Spirit-led life
Continuous / improvement	Knowledge	Stability
Cooperation	Leadership	Standardization
Coordination	Love / romance	Status
Creativity	Loyalty	Strength
Customer satisfaction	Maximum utilization (of time / resources)	Success; a will to succeed
Decisiveness	Meaning	Systemization
Delight of being / joy	Merit	Teamwork
Democracy	Money	Timeliness
Discipline	Openness	Tolerance
Discovery	Patriotism	Tradition
Diversity	Peace / non violence	Tranquility
Ease of use	Perfection	Trust
Efficiency	Personal growth	Truth
Family feeling	Pleasure	Unity
	Power	Variety
	Practicality	Wisdom
	Prosperity / wealth	

1. Write down your three most meaningful, purposeful, and exciting verbs here:

_____

_____

_____

Below is a list of core values. Pick the three that most attract you. Then, from there pick the one that most speaks of you. What do you stand for? What principle, cause, value, or purpose would you be willing to defend to the death or devote your life to? For example, some people's key phrase or value might be *joy, service, justice, family, creativity, freedom, equality, faith*, or *excellence*. What is your core? Write the word below (don't worry if you have more than one word, write them down; this maybe a process that will take time).

Mold motivate	Promise	Respect	Team
Move	Promote	Restore	Touch
Negotiate	Provide	Return	Trade
Nurture Open	Pursue	Revise	Translate
Organize	Realize	Sacrifice	Travel
Participate	Receive	Safeguard	Understand
Pass	Reclaim	Satisfy	Use
Perform	Reduce	Save	Utilize
Persuade	Refine	Sell	Validate
Play	Reflect	Serve	Value
Possess	Reform	Share	Venture
Practice	Regards, relate	Speak	Verbalize
Praise	Relax Release	Stand	Volunteer
Prepare	Rely	Summon	Work
Present	Remember	Support	Worship
Produce	Renew	Surrender	Write
Progress	Resonate	Sustain	Yield
		Take care, tap	

2.   Write down your one core value here:

Below is a list of groups and/or causes. Pick the three that most attract you. Then, from there, pick the one that most speaks of you. Pick the one group, entity, or cause you would most like to help or impact in a positive way. Write down that cause, entity, or group's name here. (Again, don't worry if you have more than one word, write them down; this may be a process that will take time.)

Environment	Advertising	Psychology
Family issues	Spirituality	Movies
Education	The ill and disabled	Design
Media	Public safety	Sports
Health care	Human development	Food
Elderly	Infants	Computer technology
Children	Child protection	Administration
The Poor	Child care	Management
The Homeless	Home health care	Construction
Immigration	Tourism	Travel
Energy	Defense	Finance
Agriculture	Space exploration	Real estate
Justice system	Animal care	Printing & publishing
Parks & recreation	Labour relations	Religion
Veterans	Literacy	Community development
Nutrition	Border issues	Reproductive issues
Law	Civil rights issues	Research
Politics	Sexuality issues	Biotech
Youth	Fashion	Women's issues
Business	Art	Gardening
Non-profit agencies	Books / literature	Broadcasting
Churches	Music	News
Engineering	Drama	Journalism
Science	Language	Performing arts

3. Write down your group or cause here:

_____

_____

_____

Putting it all together:
My mission is to:

1. _____,_____, and _____
    (Your three verbs)

2. _____
    (Your core value or values)
    to, for, or with

3. _____
    (Group/cause which most moves/excites you)

Remember, these exercises are just a start towards revealing your purpose and the answers are not set in stone. We are on a journey of faith and life, and as you gain wisdom and knowledge, your thoughts on your purpose may grow and evolve.

Take the time to go back over the past days relating to your Purpose/Calling. As you review all the answers to the activities work on creating a Life Mission Statement. Use the previous mission statements I provided as a template. And just so you know, I practice what I preach, here is mine; "*I educate people on how to be leaders not followers–thorough the life choices they make!*"

Talk Time

 Mother's Question: Were there other words that ran through your mind while reading the words above? Write these words down as well, they may be more clues to finding your purpose.

 Daughter's Question: Were there other words that ran through your mind while reading the words above? Write these words down as well, they may be more clues to finding your purpose.

Agreement: We (your signatures) _____ and _____ agree to respect and appreciate our differences.

Prayer: Dear Heavenly Father, even as we search for our purpose/mission, we know you can change our call at any time. Help us not to be stuck where you do not want us. Amen.

Finding Your Purpose/Calling
Part 5

I have fought the good fight, I have finished the
race, and I have remained faithful.

2 Timothy 4:7–8 (NLT)

There is much more to this treasure hunt for your purpose than I could ever come close to sharing with you in
this devotional. I believe finding out that God has created
you for something only you can do is empowering and
will help you to engage your focus on more than just what
today may bring.

The previous questions are only a start to your journey in discovering your purpose. I would like to tell you
something. If I had it to do all over again, I would journal
all my life, and then read what I had written so I could see
my purpose come to life.

Your life's call is important—so important that God
gave it only to you with the belief that you would live it
out. Yes, it is true that God is powerful enough and large
enough that if you miss your call, he can, and will, have
someone step into it. Although the way you live out your
call is unique and what you do always affects your circle of
influence. Someone else may not be able to touch the people you were to touch in just the way your life would have.

What you do with your life always affects more than you. Sorry, ladies, I know it is a lot of pressure! I also know that God has, and will, give you all that you need to accomplish what he has placed you on this earth to do.

Mom, something to consider: I believe this generation is not being told that they have a purpose. Our society promotes a self-centered lifestyle: it's my way or the highway, climb to the top of the ladder stepping on whoever gets in your way. Our kids will go through their early adult life searching for what they need when what they need is to find out what they have to give to others. Their purpose is not about them or what they want. It is about what they have been gifted with from God to bless others.

Ladies, you both have a purpose, and you are never too old or too young to find it and live it out.

Talk Time

 Mother's Question: What's something new that these last few days of the devotional have shown you?

 Daughter's Question: What is something you can do right now to work towards finding or living out your purpose/call?

Agreement: We (your signatures) _____ and _____ agree to help each other find and then live out our God-given purpose/calling.

Prayer: Dear Heavenly Father, thank you for giving us a purpose to live out on this Earth. Help us to live it out. Amen.

Your Destiny Cannot be Destroyed

> To the angel of the church in Philadelphia write:
> These are the words of him who is holy and true,
> who holds the key of David. What he opens no
> one can shut, and what he shuts no one can open.
> I know your deeds. See, I have placed before you
> an open door that no one can shut.
>
> Revelations 3:7–8 (NIV)

The following are my random thoughts about the above topic.

What God opens before us, no man can shut.

Remember to not focus on other people's actions. It is not their actions that will determine where you go. No other person controls your destiny. What God has destined for you cannot be taken away by man.

No one else can take away what God has given you, but you may forfeit it.

Because God has created your destiny for you and wants you to have it does not automatically mean that you will have it. You must discipline yourself to be faithful in the place where God has called you and placed you.

Because God has placed an open door before us does not mean there will not be opposition.

We have an enemy in Satan, and he will attempt to destroy what God has planned for you. Make sure you are prepared by putting on the armor of God every day. There is safety in your mom and dad, and, Mom, in your husband. Those in authority over us need to fight in the spiritual realm for us. Ask them to pray for you and protect you.

Destiny is not something you can force your way into.

You may seemingly have been passed by, you are not in the place of popularity, people do not notice you, but God knows who you are. He knows the purposes he has for you. Submit to God and those whom he has placed over you, and in his time, he will bring you into your destiny.

Continually check your heart.

Coming into your destiny depends on your heart more than your circumstances. Your heart attitude, more than anything, will open up your destiny.

As we trust God, he will always make a way for us to overcome any obstacles. God's plan for us is not that we do not face challenges, but that he would be glorified through the challenges we go through. God's promise is that when he places an open door in front of us, he will provide what is necessary for us to go through it. God does not give us opportunity and then frustrate us by not making it impossible for us to go through.

> Ask and it will be given to you; seek and you will find; knock and the door will be opened to you. For everyone who asks receives; he who seeks finds; and to him who knocks, the door will be opened.
>
> Matthew 7:7–8 (NIV)

God will not give you a road map for the year ahead and say, "Go do it." He will walk before you each day and say, "Walk with me; we can get there together." Stay close to your Shepherd, and it will be a great life of growth in every way.

The man who enters by the gate is the shepherd of his sheep. The watchman opens the gate for him, and the sheep listen to his voice. He calls his own sheep by name and leads them out. When he has brought out all his own, he goes on ahead of them, and his sheep follow him because they know his voice.

John 10:2–4 (NIV)

Talk Time

Mother's Question: Is God calling you? Do you hear his voice? Share what he has asked you to do. Are you allowing those in authority over you to fulfill their role?

Daughter's Question: What do you think God's voice sounds like, and have you heard it? Are you allowing those in authority over you to fulfill their role?

Agreement: We (your signatures) _____ and _____ agree to focus on God and walk with him into our destinies.

Prayer: Dear Heavenly Father, help us to quiet ourselves, to be still, and know that you are God. Also, help us to follow the voice of our Shepherd and to allow those in authority to fulfill their role. Amen.

Notes

_____

_____

_____

_____

_____

_____

_____

_____

_____

_____

_____

_____

_____

_____

_____

_____

_____

First Impressions

Look beneath the surface so you can judge correctly.

John 7:24 (NLT)

When someone forms a first impression of you, they get to see just a sample of who you are. Unfortunately, to them, that represents 100 percent of who you are, especially if they never get the chance to know you better. This is why first impressions are so important. There is a great book I read called *First Impressions* by Ann Demarais, PhD, and Valerie White, PhD.

In their first chapter, "What You Don't Know about How Others See You," they have a test that is similar to the one on the next page. I have altered it according to my thoughts. Take it for yourself and see where your natural tendencies fall in making a good first impression.

If I meet someone new, I	Usually	Sometimes	Rarely	
I am aware of my body language; I lean toward others when engaging in a conversation.				P
I talk so fast that they can't keep up.				N
I listen intently, shutting out the surrounding noises.				P
I share more information about myself than I should in a conversation.				N
I make myself look important by telling them everything I do.				N
I ask many questions about them.				P
I search for things we have in common.				P
Freedom of speech is important, so whatever I believe, I need them to know that.				N

If you answered usually to the questions with a P (positive first impressions), you are doing well with your first impressions. Remember, great first impressions take work, so keep at it.

If you answered usually to the questions with an N (negative first impressions), consider this saying by Zig Ziglar: "People don't care how much you know until they know how much you care." You can only get to the place of showing how much you care if they want to meet with you again.

We will look more into this topic tomorrow, but before I close, I want to leave you with a thought. Psychological research has shown that people weigh initial information much more heavily than later information when they evaluate people.

So how important do you think first impressions are?

Talk Time

 Mother's Question: Is it hard for you to communicate with someone the first time you meet? Do you struggle with what to say or do?

 Daughter's Question: Same question as Mom. Is it hard for you to communicate with someone the first time you meet? Do you struggle with what to say or do?

Agreement: We (your signatures) _____ and _____ agree to work on our first impressions. We agree to always try to make our best first impressions, remembering that we are showing people the light of Christ through us.

Prayer: Dear Heavenly Father, show us how to be genuine and be who we really are and to know we are worth getting to know. Amen.

Notes

_____

_____

_____

_____

_____

_____

_____

_____

_____

_____

_____

_____

_____

_____

_____

Secrets to Making a Good First Impression

> Words from a wise man's mouth are gracious, but
> a fool is consumed by his own lips.
>
> Ecclesiastes 10:12 (NIV)

The best communicators have learned that it is not all about them. People don't care how much you know until they know how much you care. When meeting someone for the first time, it is not so much that they see you, but that you see them.

Did you know that it takes forty seconds for someone to know that you are glad to be with them?

These are stages we may go through when first meeting someone:

- Creating a picture of who we are, we draw the picture with words we say about ourselves. Be careful whom you paint yourself to be; if this relationship goes further, you may have to live up to that initial picture.

- The next thing we do is try to get to know the other person; unfortunately, judgments have a tendency to creep in. We tend to start thinking about whether or not we like this person. May I suggest this to be a time of grace? Everyone finds it hard meeting new people and they are often nervously trying to get you to not reject them.

• Then you move to thinking about, *I wonder if this person even likes me.* We become suspicious and often start trying harder to make them like us. When really, if they can't like us for who we are, perhaps they should just be an acquaintance.

• Once you are working toward more than a first meeting, you will start to realize what that person thinks of themselves. This may be a ministry opportunity for you or this person may be someone who is going to bring something into your life. For example, you may struggle with something at school (or Mom, at work or home), and God has sent this person with a message to help.

• Now, after all this is said, I believe every meeting in your life is a divine appointment, and you should treat each meeting in that way. Never leave a first meeting without taking it to prayer to find out what God had in mind for you or the other person.

Just a note: when we are young, we are so afraid we will have no friends, so we try to make friends with everyone. Believe me when I say, not everyone was brought into your life to share it with you, and some of them won't be life-giving to you. Enjoy the "get acquainted" time, but don't rush into a friendship.

Talk Time

Mother's Question: What type of first impressions do you want to make? When someone leaves after first meeting you, what would you like them to say?

Daughter's Question: Same question: What type of first impressions do you want to make? When someone leaves after first meeting you, what would you like them to say?

Agreement: We (your signatures) _____ and _____ agree to see each meeting as a divine appointment created for God's purposes. To see everyone we meet through the eyes of Christ.

Prayer: Dear Heavenly Father, show us how to look at the people we meet as your children and to remember that you have arranged each meeting in our lives. Amen.

Notes

Choosing Your Friends

Do not be misled: "Bad company corrupts good character."

1 Corinthians 15:33–34 (NIV)

It may seem like you do not really choose your friends—you just end up being friends with those you go to school with, people at your church, or those in your neighbourhood. This tends to be more common with young people. Everyone my granddaughter meets, she claims as her best friend.

Perhaps I can challenge you and say that we do pick and choose our friends; we do not have to be friends with everyone who talks to us. For starters, what if I was to say, "God should be a part of the process for choosing your friends"? I know you cannot just say to someone you meet, "Let me take some time in prayer and ask God if I can be your friend." But, what if we did take the time to ask and not only, "Is this friendship for me, Lord?" but how about, "Is there a purpose for this friendship?"

As I age, I look back over my life and I can see where God had placed people (friends) at the right time and place in my life. Either there was growth for me or for them.

There were also some very good friends in my life that spoke into my life about relationships that were taking me in the wrong direction and were unhealthy. I have watched people I love be torn apart over relationships that they should never have been a part of.

I think if we have a place of reference for what a good friend is, we can eliminate a lot of hardship.

Here are some things that represent a good friend:

- Your friend allows you to have many friends.

- Honesty is important in a friendship.

- Friends sometimes hurt each other, but they can apologize and forgive.

- Friends should influence you in a positive way.

- Friends should be caring and when possible available—the gift of your time and genuine concern is part of a good friendship.

- A good friendship will make you feel good about yourself.

- A good friend is willing to make sacrifices; they will go the extra mile.

- A good friend will be loyal to you; they will not go behind your back. They will hold your integrity in high esteem.

- Truthfulness is an important part of trust—to have a friend you trust, you will need them to always be honest.

- A good friend will do what it takes to keep you safe in body, spirit, and mind.

After reading these points, how many good friends would you say you have?

Some points to ponder: if you have a friend and there is something happening in their life that worries you, please share it with an adult you trust. In other words, care enough for them that their whole life is important to you, not just what they may think of you tomorrow. Moms, at times, this may apply to relationships you have as well. Lead those friends to help. Pray for the Holy Spirit to intervene, but speak the truth to them in love.

Spending time together will help you get to know your friends well enough so that you can perhaps feel comfortable sharing your feelings. Until you have a sense of trust, it is better to wait to share important things with them.

The friends you have are completely up to you. It is your choice. You cannot say, "My friends chose me". In fact, they may have approached you or pursued you, but the ultimate choice is yours. That's right, not even your parents'. Just yours. So choose wisely. Moms, you too! Moms, modeling what a good friend is helps your daughter to know what good friendships are and also how to be a good friend.

Talk Time

 Mother's Question: Were there people you made your friends that you wish you had not? Do you have a good friend now?

 Daughter's Question: Are there friendships you have now that may need to be re-examined?

Agreement: We (your signatures) _____ and _____ agree to make friendships an important part of our lives. And agree to work at our own mother-daughter friendship.

Prayer: Dear Heavenly Father, thank you for our friends. Help us to be a godly influence and to not allow bad influences and deception into our relationships. Amen.

Being a Good Friend

A friend is always loyal, and a brother is born to help in time of need.

Proverbs 17:17 (NLT)

Yesterday, the qualities I listed told you what good friends are; these also apply to being a good friend. I do not know if you are anything like me, but I find taking a friendship to the good/best friend level difficult. I also believe there are too many people we call our good/best friends when perhaps they are just simply an acquaintance or maybe just a friend. The energy and time it takes to be a good/best friend would indicate to me that having many is impossible.

I think classifying your friends may be helpful. Here is a brief explanation of what the different types of friendships may be:

- An acquaintance—someone you may see in a group setting, but, never alone. Or you may see them only at certain times, and perhaps only in passing. There is not a deep connection with these people. These types of friendships deserve your kindness and encouragement, but until they cross the line into being a good/best friend, you need to guard what you share with them and how much time you spend with them and what you do for them.

- A friend—is someone whom you would spend time with occasionally, but with whom you share very little about your life. Most of your interactions are on the superficial level.

- A good/best friend—someone to whom all the good friend rules apply; be careful, though, because as I said before, you can never be a good/best friend to everyone. It would take way too much time and emotional/ spiritual energy. Choose your best friends wisely; those who bring out the best in you and you bring out the best in them.

- Boyfriends—now I am not saying boyfriend. Guys should be more like an acquaintance or a brother. The only guy who should be your good/ best friend is the guy who is going to become your husband. I'll go into more detail on my thoughts about that in the dating section of the next devotional series.

Please remember when I say that you must watch how much you do for people. I am in no way saying that giving should be done only for our true best friends. We are to always have a desire for serving others. I am saying; if we are always giving, there will never be enough of us to go around, and if we are never on the receiving end, we will be giving from a place of emptiness. This is not what God wants. He clearly said, "Love your neighbor as yourself."

Talk Time

 Mother's Question: Talk about a time you invested into a good friendship and the wonderful experiences that came from that.

 Daughter's Question: Who is your best friend? How does your friendship measure up with the qualities listed earlier?

Agreement: We (your signatures) _____ and _____ agree to make an effort to be the best friend we can be, especially to each other.

Prayer: Dear Heavenly Father, show us how to be a friend like Jesus was. Show us where there may be areas we need to improve on the effort we put into our friendships. Amen.

Notes

_____

_____

_____

_____

_____

_____

_____

_____

_____

_____

_____

_____

_____

_____

Friendships with Guys

Treat younger women with all purity as you would your own sisters.

1 Timothy 5:2 (NLT)

Okay, right off the bat, I can guess what you are thinking. She is going to say what every older person (watch older, I am still young at heart) says, "No guy friends." Well, you know what I really think? You should have guy friends. Otherwise, how are you going to learn how guys think or act? Okay, Mom, relax. I have some areas of concern myself. So let's discuss this between grown women.

Let's start by defining a grown woman's relationship with a male friend? A mature friendship with a male starts with understanding a few very specific characteristics of how males act.

God created men to be physical first and emotional second. In such, the physical aspect of a relationship with a guy has to be much different than with your girlfriends. This means hugging, holding hands, back rubs, and any physical touch needs to be reserved for the one and only guy. I need you to understand that the physical first trait is not the fault of guys. It is an inherent trait set by God for them to desire physical touch. With men, young or old, they think logically and need to understand your boundaries in a logical way right off the bat. All men

151

want to have clear instructions. You will hear it from men as you age, "Please! I cannot read your mind. Just tell me what you want!" Men need clear and concise information. Set the rules for the relationship right from the get-go.

We women tend to think and act through our emotions; because of this, enforcing boundaries may be difficult. We have a fear of rejection that lies below the surface of those emotions. Please hear me, "If you are rejected for setting and enforcing boundaries, the relationship you are in is not healthy and mutual respect is not evident. This will not get better with time. As the old saying goes, "Give an inch they will take a mile."

For your reputation and your safety, time alone with a guy should be very well thought out and, perhaps, not even allowed. One thing you will find as you grow older is that most of what you do will be done on an emotional basis. You will find it hard to separate your feelings from your logic. God has designed you to desire love. This means you will do things for love that you would never do for logic. Being alone with a boy could put you in a position of not being able to think logically.

There is also your reputation. This is something only you can protect. Yes, only you. You need to guard it with a vengeance. Your reputation will take you places in your life that nothing else can.

Guys can be friends; just make sure they understand the rules before you get involved. And for the guy's sake, please do not lead them on. This devotional is written for girls, but I would put the same information out to the guys. Just because they are more logical thinkers does not mean they do not feel. They have feelings too. You need to guard and protect their feelings as well by not flirting and leading them on.

Just one more tip. Moms, if you don't want your daughters hugging their guy friends, perhaps you shouldn't either.

Talk Time

 Mother's Question: Talk to your daughter about her reputation and her desire to be loved. Only you can explain it in the way she will understand.

 Daughter's Question: Discuss with your mom how you feel about having guys as friends.

Agreement: We (your signatures) _____ and _____ agree to protect each other from relationships that would harm us or destroy our reputation.

Prayer: Dear Heavenly Father, help us to set good boundaries in all our relationships. Amen.

Notes

_____

_____

_____

_____

_____

_____

_____

_____

_____

_____

_____

_____

_____

_____

What Guys Say About Friendships

I am a friend to anyone who fears you–anyone who obeys your commandments.

Psalms 119:63 (NLT)

Girls, do you ever wonder what guys think about friendships in general and about having them with girls?

Below are samplings of questions asked of our Guys' Panel: (Guy's Panel is comprised of a group of guys who have volunteered at our retreats at one time or another; they too are on the chastity challenge). These questions were asked by the girls who have attended our retreats. After the questions are collected from the girls, they are given to the guys who in turn take the Saturday afternoon to discuss and pray over the answers.

1. Why do guys seem to not want to be just friends? When you say no when they ask you out, they won't talk to you anymore.

> It gets awkward.
>
> We don't handle rejection well.
>
> We have difficulties in being just friends.
>
> You can't only be "just friends" with a guy.

2. Why does your personality change when you're with your friends?

> We act differently around different people (different comfort levels).
>
> Not all of us are like that.
>
> We could ask you the same question.

3. Why are you guys so nice when your friends are not around, but when they are, you turn back into jerks?

> We don't know, none of us are jerks.
>
> We suspect that those guys don't truly respect you.

4. How do your relationships with your guy friends and girl friends differ?

> Guys are more relaxed, you can joke around, be more physical.
>
> With girls, we are more self-conscious and sensitive.

5. Why can't guys who like you just be friends with you?

> They feel awkward; they're afraid of rejection.
>
> Peer pressure. They think that if you won't be their girlfriend, you don't want to be their friend.

Guys look for friends or for girlfriends. The ones who are looking to be friends will be okay with being your friend.

6. When we tell you we just want to be friends, why are you so persistent about dating?

Sometimes, when someone thinks they are popular and you won't go out with them, they feel rejected or challenged and push further.

Sometimes, when girls say they just want to be friends, they are just playing hard-to-get and want you to push harder.

If a guy really likes a girl, it's really hard just to be around them as friends. So guys either hang around, hoping it will change, or don't hang around at all.

Seeing these questions and answers, perhaps we could say that guys don't always think like us, and if that is the case, maybe, just maybe, we should ask a guy's opinion about certain things. Girls, a caution, make sure when you look for a guy's opinion that you find someone you can trust to answer honestly. The best place to start would be with your dad or older brothers. If there is no male role model in your life, then ask your mom to help you find someone with whom to discuss these questions: a pastor, priest, youth leader, an uncle, or someone that can be trusted.

Talk Time

 Mother's Question: Did you find any of the guys' answers a little surprising? Why?

 Daughter's Question: Same question: Did you find any of the guys' answers a little surprising? Why?

Agreement: We (your signatures) _____ and _____ agree to always remember to ask questions and not to assume we know what people (especially guys) are thinking or feeling.

Prayer: Dear Heavenly Father, thank you for creating men differently from women, so that together we can be all you have planned for us to be. Amen.

Letting Go of Unhealthy Friendships

Fools have no interest in understanding; they only want to air their own opinions.

Proverbs 18:2 (NLT)

It takes many learned skills to make and maintain a friendship; it also takes many skills to end a friendship. Friendships that do not provide you growth or damage who you are should be let go. I know you are thinking, "What about the other side of that where the Bible says 'love your enemies?' How are we to do that if we let them go?" Let me be clearer: you never should truly let anyone go as they have crossed your path for a reason, but you can distance yourself from them and then pray for them.

Sometimes we get into or stay in friendships that are unhealthy.

How do you know you should let a friend go?

Ask yourself these questions, does he or she:

- Consistently hurt your feelings?

- Chip away at your self-esteem?

- Spoil happy times with a bad attitude?

- Make you feel physically or emotionally ill?

- Waste your time by not showing up or calling when they said they would?

- Consume your time and energy by sucking you into their dramas and bad habits?

- Demand too much of your time and/or try to limit your contact with others?

- Offer friendship only at their convenience and express little interest in what's going on in your life?

- Get in the way of your personal, emotional, and spiritual growth?

- Speak behind your back, spread untruths, or exaggerate truth for their gain?

- Always try to one-up you?

- Speak badly about your other friends or your family?

- Do things you know you would never do or the people you care about would never approve of?

- Or if you have started to wonder why you are feeling resentful toward a so-called friend, is it really worth the investment of your time or energy?

Now if you found yourself saying "yes" to many—or most—of the above questions, it may be time to rethink those friendships.

A few helpful tips to keep in mind when confronting issues in a friendship:

- Keep the focus on you. Always use "I statements" when addressing issues. A simple way to remember this is by using statements like "I feel" instead of "You make me feel." An example would be: "When you say _____ (fill in the blank), I feel bad about who I am as a person." Not: "You make me feel bad." Another example using a time issue: "We had agreed to meet at 8. It is now 8:30 and I have missed out on other plans." If you are separating the action from the person, you say, "When you do this, I (not you make me) feel you don't value my time.

- "Speak the truth." Always stand firm on your standards/values. Remember though to speak the truth in love not conviction. An example of speaking the truth in love would be: "Angie, you are an amazing person in so many ways, but the truth is I cannot be around you if you are hanging out in bars or with guys who are using drugs. If there is ever a time you want to just have a coffee together, give me a call."

- The other area where we tend to go wrong is using the words like *always* or *never*. People neither *never* nor *always* do something. Even if it feels like never or always, make sure you say often or sometimes.

- Distancing yourself is a way to release a friendship that is unhealthy? To make that transition easier find things you like to do that feed your mind, body, and soul. Fill your time with these activities and then when asked what you are doing tonight, you can say, "you have plans." Remember, plans can be just to go home and do nothing or to wait for someone else to call. Enough times of saying no will usually tell the story.

- Remember never to be cruel; do all things in love.

- If you struggle in any of the communication areas I shared above seek help from someone you trust. Communicating difficult messages is tough for all of us, but to avoid or shade information so that we are liked will only serve to damage us and our relationship.

Talk Time

 Mother's Question: Was there a time in your life when you had to let go of a friendship? How did that go? Is there someone you can think of that should be let go of and prayed for?

 Daughter's Question: Is there a friend you can think of that should be let go of and prayed for? Can you set a plan to work that through?

Agreement: We (your signatures) _____ and _____ agree to trust each other's desire for our well-being when we discuss who should be our friends and who should not.

Prayer: Dear Heavenly Father, help us to choose our friends wisely and to pray for those we may need to let go of. Amen.

Purity of Your Friendships and Friends

Walk with the wise and become wise; associate with fools and get in trouble.

Proverbs 13:20 (NLT)

"You are who you hang out with." Heard this before? You may be thinking. "No! you are who you are, right?" Maybe you could ask yourself this: do I act the same way with my friends as I do everywhere else? For example; when you are hanging out with your family or when you are at youth group or in church. Are you the same as you are when you are hanging out with your friends? If you answered, "No, sometimes, I am different." This would lead me to believe that at times you are who you hang out with. For instance, does your language or the way you say things change (and this is minimal)? Where do you see the change? Do you perhaps try things your friends are doing just to fit in? Will you smoke, drink, do drugs? Will you date just to be like your friends?

What if you are hanging around with a group of friends that are experimenting in areas that are unhealthy or unsafe such as, lying, dangerous acts (like chicken) or stealing? If this might be the case, you need to know the consequences that may come with just being there.

Unfortunately, people will start to think differently of you. Your parents, teachers, youth group, any of the people in your healthy relationships, are they thinking, "You must be doing what they are doing." You must be careful as association creates labels, and you could ruin your reputation. Ask yourself, "What do I want people to think of my character?"

Let's say, you are all in a group and something happens, such as one of them going into a convenience store, and while there robs it. All the sudden the alarm goes off. This may be extreme, but I want you to visualize worst-case scenarios. The police come, and all of you are taken to the station. This my friend is called guilt by association. Unfair maybe, but true. What if you are in a car with someone who is drinking and driving, there is an accident and someone is killed. You are innocent, technically, as you were not driving, but remember, you did not take a stand for what was right. Extreme, maybe, but it happens more often than you know.

What I want most is for you to see, that unfortunately people associate your character with those you surround yourself with. Also, unless you can say that you, beyond a shadow of a doubt, can never be persuaded to do what others around you are doing, you may find yourself doing something you regret, all because you hung out with the wrong crowd.

Find good friends who accept you for who you are and won't try to mold you to fit in with the crowd. Your reputation and character may not seem like a big deal now, but you may carry some of those wrong choices into your future.

Moms, this day maybe hit hard for the girls, but you may need to rethink whom you associate yourself with. Your kids are watching. A caution: this doesn't mean you don't do ministry to those less fortunate. Jesus hung out with sinners, but for a reason. Make sure to check your heart.

Talk Time

Mother's Question: Did you act differently around your friends when you were young? Do you tend to change who you are when you're around your friends now?

Daughter's Question: Do you tend to change who you are when you're around your friends?

Agreement: We (your signatures) _____ and _____ agree to tell each other when we see changes in our character when we are around certain friends. Then to help each other make the right decision through loving words.

Prayer: Dear Heavenly Father, we pray for all the people that will come into our lives, that they are all positive influences. If they are not, we pray that you would help us to see it and give us the strength to let them go. We pray for all who struggle and do not know you. Lord, show us how to share our faith with our friends. Amen.

Notes

_____

_____

_____

_____

_____

_____

_____

_____

_____

_____

_____

_____

_____

_____

_____

Dangers of Being a People Pleaser

> Love the Lord your God with all your heart and
> with all your soul and with all your mind and with
> all your strength. The second is this: 'Love your
> neighbour as yourself. There is no commandment
> greater than these.
>
> Mark 12:30–31 (NIV)

The bible tells us that as followers of Christ, we are to
love everyone, even our enemies. There is a danger in loving everyone (even our enemies), when we equate love
with doing things for others. We are not to perform acts
of service or give of ourselves to the degree of making
ourselves unhealthy. However it does mean to act in love
in everything we do, and sometimes, that means doing
nothing, or perhaps just praying for them.

God also doesn't want us worrying about what people
think. It is more important to him that the motives for
your actions are pure and come from a heart for God.

One of the difficulties here is deciphering our motives
to know if we are pleasing people or God. If you are feeling any of the following things, you may be doing things
for people:

- You have a loss of personal identity.

- You have a loss of personal rights.
- You are being taken advantage of.
- You have little or no personal time.
- You feel burned-out.
- You fear a loss of approval.
- You fear rejection.
- You feel no sense of personal worth.
- There is a chronic state of being unappreciated.

If you see yourself in any of these, you may have a tendency to please people. It is difficult to change this behavior as it involves how we feel about ourselves. Be encouraged. You have already made the first step by recognizing the need to change. The next step is going to be the hardest: getting over the fear that if you change, people won't like you. You need to know that not everyone is going to like you and that is okay. If you have to do something for someone to make them like you, they are not true friends. People should love you for who you are, not what you can do.

To stop being a people-pleaser, you need to learn an important skill: the art of communicating the word "no." You need to be able to say it in a way that doesn't sound harsh or pointed. Here are some simple tips: rehearse and practice saying no to people you have a safe relationship with. Say "no" to easy things at first such as "No, I don't want a piece of that chocolate cake." Get in front of a mirror and practice saying "no". Then, when the times come for you to say "no," you will be on your way to feeling comfortable with your ability.

Never forget: most important is to pray and ask God to help you. If you know he loves you, no matter what happens, you will be able to overcome anything—even someone not liking you. I promise. If you know his love, there is no greater.

Talk Time

 Mother's Question: I know for a fact that as a mother, wife, and in the many other roles you play, you will have a hard time saying "no" to people. Talk to your daughter about this.

 Daughter's Question: What are some of the things you have a hard time saying "no" to?

Work together. Practice and prepare to say "no" so that when either of you needs to, it won't be difficult.

Agreement: We (your signatures) _____ and _____ agree to help each other to know when it is healthy to say "no" and to help each other be accountable in doing so.

Prayer: Dear Heavenly Father, help us to see that you love us and that we are to be pleasing to you, not to man. Amen.

Notes

Importance of Your Family Relationships

Here am I, and the children God has given me.

Hebrews 2:13 (NIV)

It may be that you want to share this day's writing as a family devotional. Mom, perhaps it might be helpful to discuss this day first with your husband; this will ensure that your kids see that their parents are on the same page.

Believe it or not, God chose the family you would be raised in; yes, even you, Mom and Dad. If God put you in your family of origin, he knew that was where he needed you, and what he needed to have for your purpose on Earth to start to be cultivated. Mom and Dad, if you happen to come from a dysfunctional home, God's intent was not to see you suffer. He gave us freedom of choice and your parents made incorrect choices. I can assure you that his plan for your family was different. Remember, however, God takes what Satan meant for harm and turns it to good. I have also come to believe that perhaps some children are put into struggling families because God needs them there to make a difference for their family.

As a family, God has a mission for you. Not only is your family a place to cultivate your personal purpose, there is a purpose for you as a family unit. As a life coach,

I speak to women especially, about taking the focus off micromanaging their family. I help them to take their focus off time spent just getting through the week and functioning as a family. We dive into looking at why God has placed you together as a family unit.

One of my favorite tools for looking at this is Steven Covey's *7 Habits of Highly Effective Families*. He has devoted a part of his book to creating a family mission statement (what God wants for you as a family).

Below are a few questions from his book. You may find them helpful in designing your family mission statement:

> A family mission statement is a combined, unified expression from all family members of what your family is all about—what it really wants to do or be and the principle you choose to govern your family life.

What is the purpose of our family? What is this family about? What are our highest priorities and goals? What are some ways as a family you could accomplish those goals?

Pose these questions to each member of your family, have them write their answers, and then share those answers with each other.

The most important rule in sharing these questions is that there are no right or wrong answers. You must be open to all suggestions and find ways to include everyone's valuable input. It will take more than one discussion to find your family mission statement. This exercise requires time with God. He is our designer. He knows the purpose he has created a family for.

Note: do not forget to ask the why question: "Why do you feel this is important?"

Remember, this is just a starting point for designing your family mission statement. Take time in prayer and discussion to mold your mission statement into a solid foundation of truths that your family can stand on. As time goes on, your mission statement may alter slightly according to the members of your family aging and changing, but the values and principles will always remain the same.

Talk Time

 Mother's Question: I leave you with the questions above to answer.

 Daughter's Question: I leave you with the questions above to answer.

Agreement: We (your signatures) _____ and _____ agree to discuss and pray over our family mission. To actively live out what God has planned for us as a family.

Prayer: Dear Heavenly Father, thank you for placing us as a family. Help us to see the call you have for us as a family and to live it out. Amen.

Notes

Understanding Your Role in Your Family

My child, if your heart is wise, my own heart will rejoice!

Proverbs 23:15 (NLT)

If what I said yesterday is true, and I believe it to be, our families were designed by God. He knit us together as a family.

Our role as parents has been divinely designed, but is it easy? No way. Most of us as parents wish our children would have come with instructions. Each child-parent relationship is so diverse; no two are ever the same. We genuinely desire a connected relationship with our kids, but we both have to do our part.

In the early years from the age of about ten on into the teen years, there is a separation that is taking place. Like a bird that leaves its nest, you are starting to spread your wings so you can fly solo. To parents, that letting go is one of the toughest things they will ever have to do. I have talked to many parents who share that once a child leaves home, they experience deep feelings of loss, although we are well aware that this is the process of life. When you leave, you leave a hole only you can fill.

This is a time of learning and transitioning for all of us. Not only are you learning how to leave, but we are learning how to let go. During this period of you maturing into an adult, our job as a parent is to teach you how to make good choices. Your life will be a product of the choices you make: good and bad. Even if outside influences seem to be the cause, your choice of how to respond to those influences will bring the outcome.

If your parents' role is to teach, your role in the family is to be a student, to learn how to live independently. You also have much to give to your family. As you learn and internalize experiences and information, you will have your own perspectives. It is important to share these, as you may at times be the teacher too.

Remember, love and respect is very much your responsibility. Your family is a gift, treat them as such and you will be blessed. See Exodus 20:12 and Psalms 127:3–5.

Talk Time

 Mother's Question: How do you think your parents felt when you left home? How often do you see your parents now?

 Daughter's Question: What do you think it will be like when you leave home?

Agreement: We (your signatures) _____ and _____ agree to learn to work together at slowly releasing each other to the season God has called us to.

Prayer: Dear Heavenly Father, thank you for our family and that you have created it to help us grow into the people you are calling us to be. Help us to grow closer together, even as we prepare to part. Amen.

Notes

Importance of a Strong Relationship with Your Parents

> My son, obey your father's commands, and don't neglect your mother's instruction.
>
> Proverbs 6:20 (NLT)

Your parents are your first intimate relationship. Through them, you will learn how to be in a relationship. Remember, there are never perfect relationships and certainly no perfect parents. To build a strong relationship with your parents—you have to understand—it is work. Every relationship takes work. We study and educate ourselves for years to get into the professions we want, and yet for marriage and parenting, there are no required classes or textbooks. We learn about relationships by being in them.

Being in a family is a safe place to learn about human characteristics. One of the questions I often ask my coaching clients is, "What were your parents' dreams?" It surprises me that so few of my clients know. Why is it that we do not get to know our parents as people rather than just as Mom and Dad?

I know for a fact that at your age, you are trying desperately to spread your wings and you are starting to prepare for leaving the nest. I can also promise you that this is one of the hardest things your parents will ever have to do: "Let you go." In your lifetime, which could span toward eighty years or more here on Earth, your parents have maybe eighteen years or less to prepare you for that life. Not only that, but after you are eighteen, we know our time with you will be drastically less. The thing is we enjoy our time with you.

Even when it comes to choosing a lifestyle of purity, the strength of your relationship with your parents will be a big part of the deciding factor. Your family has influence on your life more so than anyone else. Your formative years before puberty are your prime learning years. It is where the foundations for what you will believe come into place. One of the things I try to help parents understand is that they are not raising children, they are raising adults. They need to prepare you for life beyond home.

I know you cannot wait to be on your own: no rules, no curfews. I can promise you this—for the first little while when you have your freedom, the consequences of all your choices will make you set your own rules.

Today at thirty-three, my son still says, kids want to grow up too fast. Once you leave the nest, you can never go back, not as a child anyway. He misses those freedoms of childhood—not having to make the everyday decisions that have to be made by an adult or having to do the things that your mom always does (laundry, cooking, looking after you when you were sick, and oh boy, does the list go on and there is your father's list, too).

What I want to say is, enjoy this time with your parents. Exercise your independence from them slowly. If you want more freedom, show them you can handle it. Ask their advice, and even if it seems not to fit with what's popular, take it to prayer and heart. You may find their wisdom is far more beneficial than you thought. There was a speaker I once heard that said, "He did not realize how smart his parents were until he moved away and then had to move back home."

Talk Time

 Mother's Question: What is the one thing you would like your daughter to learn from you and her dad?

 Daughter's Question: What are some of the things you have already learned from your parents and what do you wish for them to teach you in the future?

Agreement: We (your signatures) _____ and _____ agree to have a teachable spirit, to praise things done well, and to help each other to change what needs to be changed.

Prayer: Dear Heavenly Father, thank you for a safe place to learn within our family units. Amen.

Notes

_____

_____

_____

_____

_____

_____

_____

_____

_____

_____

_____

_____

_____

_____

_____

_____

Importance of Your Relationship with Your Mom

May your father and mother be glad; may she who gave you birth rejoice!

Proverbs 23:25 (NIV)

This is a very hard subject for me to write about. One, because I didn't have a strong relationship with my mother, and two, I have only raised my sons, no girls, except for Laura (my little sister from Big Sisters). She spent most of her teen years home with us and is like our daughter. Translating what I have learned from raising my sons, Cory who is now thirty-three and Ian my stepson who is twenty-one, would be that your mom is a gift from God. She is your guide who directs you in the ways of womanhood. Not having a mom to guide me has really made me aware of how much daughters need their moms.

Girls, later in life, there will be actions and words you will find yourself doing and saying that you will wonder where they came from. It's like there is transference of information without even a purposeful action. I can honestly say there are traits I received from my mother even though she was rarely there. Believe me, there are some traits I wish I would have disposed of much earlier in life, but even though my mom suffered and died from alcoholism, I can still find traits she has given me that I truly value.

Your mom is going to transfer to you the characteristics of a woman: a compassionate and gentle caring heart, elegance, diplomacy, and so much more. She will teach you how to be a helpmate to your husband, how to nurture and strengthen your family, and how to set the tone for your home. The Bible expresses these roles as those of a woman, but it also states that we are to be wise in business. Trust me when I say there is glory in all roles, that of a mom who can stay home to raise her children and those who work outside of the home.

All these things can only be transferred from the mom (not always your birth mom) that your Heavenly Father has provided. He knew exactly who should play this role in your life, and it was your mom. The Bible says to honor your mother and father, and I believe that is because they were chosen just for you. I can hear you say, "But—" and I know all about "buts." I also know there is good in everything we learn, we just have to find it.

I asked a very wise woman (my daughter-in-law) what she thought was one of the most important things a mom instills in her daughter. This was her answer:

> When I think about my relationship with Madi and mine with my mom, the biggest thing that jumps out at me is the importance of individualism. My mom has spent my life looking at me through her eyes and seeing herself in me, instead of seeing me as my own person. I do it to Madi all the time. When doing homework, when playing, when dealing with her emotions, I constantly

wonder why she is doing things the way she is. That's not how I did them when I was her age, and after all, she's *my* daughter, right? So she should do it the same way I did. When I catch myself thinking these thoughts, I have to take a step back and just look at her as her own person, with her own experiences and emotions and capabilities, and respect her for her differences. Madi has this down pat of course. She sees the differences in our opinions and celebrates those differences and is proud of herself when she sees things differently, and expresses them to me, and we can have a conversation about them. I just think it's so important for a mother to look at a daughter as her own person and not the newer version of herself. Although we must all admit we are so commonly just like our mothers, that often we don't have a leg to stand on when denying we are simply the newer version. From the other side, I think it is so important for little girls to understand that they can be themselves and don't have to be their moms (written by Nici Reevers).

I have to say I completely agree with my daughter-in-law. After reading this, I thought of how I have done the same, not only with my son, but in more relationships than I would care to mention. We need to remember God has designed us all to be unique individuals.

Talk Time

 Mother's Question: What are things you remember your mom imparting to you for your journey through womanhood? What characteristics do you love in your daughter?

 Daughter's Question: What is your mom's best characteristic? In other words, what characteristic of hers would you love to model in the future?

Agreement: We (your signatures) _____ and _____ agree to see each other for the unique people God has made us to be.

Prayer: Dear Heavenly Father, thank you for creating mother-daughter relationships. Show us how to love one another for who you have created us to be. Amen.

Importance of Your Dad-Relationship

The father of godly children has cause for joy.
What a pleasure to have children who are wise.

Proverbs 23:24 (NLT)

Note: If possible, have the girls' dad join you for this day's topic. If he is joining you it would be a good idea to let him read this day's information beforehand. That way, he will be prepared for the question time.

In all the information I have read and my experiences, it has become very clear to me that a father molds the image of what a husband is to be in his daughter's life. This not only happens at childhood, but carries on into the years of courtship and marriage.

A father also will create a picture not only to his daughters, but also his sons, of what our Heavenly Father's love is like. If our fathers are absent, cruel, strict, unkind, unloving, or anything else, we will translate that into what God is like.

In an Immanuel prayer session I once attended, we were asked to close our eyes and visualize Jesus being with us. What I saw was Jesus on the cross and me below asking him for help, what entered my mind was, "How is he going to come down and help me if he is nailed to that cross?" See, my father was always pinned to his disease of alcoholism, he could never help, and it wasn't his fault. Can you see the correlation?

Growing up with a father who was plagued by alcoholism, I, in my early years, looked for a missing father's love. I tried to find it in men that were plagued by the same disease or unable to look after themselves. A father's love will protect young women from looking for love in all the wrong places.

I hope you see, Dads, the way you treat your wife is how your daughter will come to believe a man is to treat her. Take a week and seriously look at your relationship with your wife, see how you value her, and then ask yourself, "Am I the person I would want my daughter to marry?"

Fathers are also to help their daughters create healthy boundaries. Women are naturally inclined to say "yes". As a young girl learns her boundaries, it is necessary for her father at first to say "no" to all that is not pure and good for her. As she matures, you must teach her how to say it with love, respect, and conviction.

We heard this story by Bob Harrison at a leadership conference. His daughter was fifteen, and they were outside in the yard. Some guys she knew drove up, rolled down their window, and started talking to her. After a few minutes, she came over to her dad and asked him if she could go out and drive around with them. He refused, saying he didn't know them. After she told them "no", she came to her dad, very frustrated, and said to him, "Don't you trust me?" He responded by saying, "If I had a million dollars in a briefcase, would you think I was smart to hand it over to some guys I didn't know for them to drive around with it?" She said, "Of course not." He said to her, "You are far more valuable to me than a million dollars. If you want me to let you go with them, then invite them over so I can meet them and get to know them." She said to her dad, "Thank you for caring so much for me."

Your father wants you to find someone who will love you for the special, unique person that you are. He will see things in the guys you're interested in that you won't. When your father sees that someone loves and respects and cares for you as much as he does, then he feels free to release you into their care.

Be thankful that your father wants to protect you; this means he loves you!

Talk Time

Father's Question: Tell your daughter what she means to you.

 Mother's Question: What qualities of your daughter's father would you like her husband to have?

 Daughter's Question: What qualities of your dad would you like your husband to have?

Agreement: We (your signatures) _____ and _____ agree to understand that a man's job is to protect the women in his care, to cherish that and not turn it away.

Prayer: Dear Heavenly Father, thank you for creating father-daughter relationships. Show us how to love one another as the persons you created us to be. Amen.

Notes

_____

_____

_____

_____

_____

_____

_____

_____

_____

_____

_____

_____

_____

_____

_____

Importance of Your Church Family

Let's see how inventive we can be in encouraging love and helping out, not avoiding worshiping together as some do but spurring each other on, especially as we see the big day approaching.

Hebrews 10:24–25 (MSG)

After God and your family, your relationship with your church family is among the most important relationships in your life. Your church is responsible for equipping you to do the work of a saint. I know that sounds outlandish and you're thinking, *Me, a saint? No way!* The definition of a saint is a person sanctified; a holy or godly person; one eminent for piety and virtue; any true Christian, as being redeemed and consecrated to God. Okay, it is this simple: holy means set apart by God. To become a saint means to believe in all that God says and follow it. I know with work and prayer you can achieve this. This equipping is not just the job of your pastor, priest, minister, or any other leader of your church; the church family as a whole has responsibilities as well.

You start by forming relationships as a babe in children's church. With a well-run church, these are safe relationships that will start the transforming of your spirit. As you grow and move through milestones in your church life such as Sunday school and youth group, your church family is there to speak into your life. They are there to help you not only achieve and celebrate milestones in your life such as your graduation, professions, marriage, and family, but most of all to help you have an intimate relationship with God and to impart wisdom from his Word.

Next time you are surrounded by your church family, look with new eyes. They are there to mentor you and help you grow into a godly woman. There is an old saying that goes, "It takes a village to raise a child." This is so true and a part of your village is your church family.

There are women in your church that would love to be asked to be a mentor for younger women like yourself; pray and watch for these women. When you see a woman in your church that you would like to emulate, say to them, "You know I would love to be like you, would you have time for a visit so I can get to know more about you?"

Youth groups are also an important part of your spiritual growth. If your church doesn't have a youth group, ask your parents to find you one you could join.

I have a new respect for youth pastors as I have gotten to know Pastor Ryan, our church's youth pastor. Believe me when I say this: being a youth pastor is a call from God. Even though I work with youth at the R2WW, I would never have the energy, enthusiasm, or the knowledge that a youth pastor has. Pastor Ryan has come alongside us at the R2WW and taught as well as preached at our services on the Sundays. Knowing him as we do has opened our eyes to the challenges of working with youth. Your youth pastor has been called by God to be in spiritual authority over you; trust in that. Your youth pastor will, in some areas of your life, know you better than your parents as they immerse themselves in your culture and relate one-on-one with you. Trust them to speak into your life. As they have the element of maturity on their side, they will have been where you are and yet can understand from your point of view. Talk to them!

Talk Time

Mother's Question: Was there a youth leader in your past that spoke into your life? If so, what did you learn? If not, what do you wish you would have gained or learned from having a relationship with a youth leader?

Daughter's Question: Is there someone in church that you would choose as a mentor? Who and why?

Agreement: We (your signatures) _____ and _____ agree to make it a point to engage in relationships with our church family.

Prayer: Dear Heavenly Father, thank you for our pastors and the call on their lives. Help us to find spiritual relationships within our church family. Help us to be more open to being spiritual leaders and mentors in our home church. Amen.

None

Notes

Understanding Your Role in Your Church Family

> The heartfelt counsel of a friend is as sweet as perfume and incense.
>
> Proverbs 27:9 (NLT)

As you read yesterday, your church family plays a very important role in your growth. As much as they play a significant role, you also have a role to play. God doesn't look at you as a child like your parents do. He sees you as innocent, not yet corrupted by the world. As we come into adulthood, our innocence is jaded by what we know of the world. The Lord says to be in the world, not of the world. Believe me, this becomes more difficult as we live longer, or at least, that is my opinion.

When I read and study the word of God, I find all ages responsible to listen to God's call for themselves. Think of David, a young man who was anointed to be king at the young age of seventeen (although it was not until he was thirty years old that he actually became king). Think of that—would you be prepared to be Queen of Canada today? I do not believe David was alone though. There were all kinds of people who helped and provided wisdom for decisions he had to make to oversee his people and ensure his country prospered. But as king, the last say was his. I believe David spent many hours seeking counsel and spending time on his knees before God. In spite of that, David made some really horrendous mistakes in his life; God showed him what they were, but still gave him grace, helping him to carry out what he was called to do.

Not only was David royalty, but so are you. God is your king and you are his princess. As David had to seek God and godly counsel, so it is your responsibility too (you will find, that in your church family). You also need to be an example of a godly princess. This will be difficult at times, but through prayer and spending time with your king, you will learn what is expected to glorify him. Remember, there is always someone watching your example and because of that ones younger than you will follow in your footsteps (good or bad).

Your church needs you just the way you are—blemishes and all. God is speaking to your generation in a way he has not spoken to our generation. He has fresh, new, and exciting ways to show himself. Please help us to see him as you do. I believe God has a strong call on your generation. You may need to be patient with us, as people our age find it hard to change. Speak to us with respect, yet conviction, of the call God has on your life. Help us to see the revelation God has inspired you with. Do not hide from our generation the gift God is sharing with you. Also allow us to speak into your lives the wisdom we have gathered, it will help you achieve all God has for you.

Talk Time

 Mother's Question: Do you feel God has called you to some specific area in your home church? What is it, and how can you fulfill it?

 Daughter's Question: If you had something to teach to the younger or older generations at your church, what would it be?

Agreement: We (your signatures) _____ and _____ will remember that our church family watches us as role models to live by; we will endeavor to do our best to model godly principles. When we fail, we will release that to God, ask his forgiveness, and start anew.

Prayer: Dear Heavenly Father, thank you for placing us in our home church, show us how to be a blessing. Amen.

Notes

_____

_____

_____

_____

_____

_____

_____

_____

_____

_____

_____

_____

_____

_____

_____

Importance of Community

> They committed themselves to the teaching of
> the apostles, the life together, the common meal,
> and the prayers.
>
> Acts 2:42 (MSG)

We do an activity the first morning of every R2WW;
we call it the Welcome Bridge. Everyone on our volunteer team finds a partner; from there, they stand facing
each other. They then raise their arms in the air and grab
each other's hands, forming a bridge. At 8 a.m. sharp, we
open the doors to where breakfast is being served, and
we have each participant walk under the bridge. As they
walk under the bridge, our volunteers collapse their arms
and gently embrace each of them, smile, say good morning, along with a compliment if they feel led. This activity
emulates community. The bridge is an object lesson that
shows the strong support system we need to grow and
prosper in live.

Community is so important; it seems in today's culture,
we are losing our sense of community. We have become so
involved in online social networks and texting (no longer
even talking on the phone) that we are losing the human
side. We have become a high-tech, low-touch society. We
build fences around our properties to keep people out;
they used to be to keep animals and livestock in.

When was the last time you invested in your community? I openly admit my schedule is such that I do not make enough time for my neighbours or to volunteer in our community, but I do believe I am missing out. Lately, I have made a genuine effort to get to know my neighbours. I know I still need to reach out more into my community, but I am genuinely trying.

Our neighbours and communities desperately need the light of Christ, and you may be the only ray of light they see. If time commitments hold you back from spending time in your community, or you struggle with the community you are a part of, bringing light can be as simple as praying (but oh-so-powerful) for everyone in your area. Prayer walks around your neighbourhood could change the atmosphere.

God places us where we are. He always has a plan and you may be it! Or he may have someone in your community that is to touch your life in a way only they can.

Talk Time

 Mother's Question: What was your neighbourhood like when you grew up? What do you see that is so different today?

 Daughter's Question: What do you think about your neighbourhood—what do you like and what do you not like? When you are grown and married, what kind of neighbourhood do you picture yourself living in?

Agreement: We (your signatures) _____ and _____ agree to get involved in some way with our neighbours/community, if only by praying for them.

Prayer: Dear Heavenly Father, thank you for placing us in our community. Show us how to be a blessing to those who cross our path. Amen.

Notes

_____

_____

_____

_____

_____

_____

_____

_____

_____

_____

_____

_____

_____

_____

Understanding Your Role in Community

So encourage each other and build each other up,
just as you are already doing.

1 Thessalonians 5:11 (NLT)

What does your community consist of? Of course, we can say our neighbourhood, but I believe there is much more to consider. There is something called your sphere of influence. I believe this is where our community begins. So what is a sphere of influence? That is our immediate circle: friends, relatives, coworkers, acquaintances, and neighbours.

Your circle of influence is in your life for a reason, and perhaps for only a time, a day, or forever. They will all have some form of input in your life and you into theirs. Maybe you are thinking, "How can someone I see for only one hour in my whole lifetime have input into my life?" Let's see!

I want you to use your imagination for one moment and imagine you are at a fast-food restaurant. Let's think healthy, so Wendy's for a salad. Two scenarios evolve:

First one: you get up to the counter and the person serving you is way beyond giving good customer service; they are as bad as it gets. They do not smile, they do not ask what you want, they demand you tell them

what you want and hurry up because there is a line. The
people behind you do not know what is going on, but you
start to think they feel you have done something wrong
because no service person acts this way. You start to feel
like the whole world is looking at you. Now this person's
actions may affect the rest of your day, and you, in turn
unknowingly, may lash out at others; they too will have
no idea why, so once again, the cycle continues.

Second scenario: a cute guy is at the counter, and he
smiles when he takes your order and says something like,
"It is nice to have you come to Wendy's today, I hope you
come back." You now feel validated, and if you are like
me, kind of special because someone was thankful I was
there, and that someone was a cute guy. Now remember, I
am married to an amazing man, so when I talk about this
cute guy, I am thinking like you.

Even the smallest of things could influence how we
act, because not only do we internalize them (and sometimes we let them fester to the point of being unhealthy),
but we also project them onto others.

I hope these two scenarios help you to see why you
need to be aware of what is feeding you from the outside
world. You cannot always choose your community, but
it is your responsibility to guard what you allow to enter
your heart, mind, and soul. It is always your choice of how
you let others' actions affect you, and you are responsible
for your attitude and actions toward others.

Reading the Word of God regularly coupled with
prayer will provide protection for you against the negative or unhealthy words and actions of others. There is
a great song Laura brought to my attention, "Garbage

In, Garbage Out" by Christian sisters, Tal and Acacia. Listening to it may be enlightening.

Remember, you are part of a community and have a sphere of influence for a reason. Do what you can to make it a better place. Keep in mind, it is not all about you and how you feel; it is more about how you make others feel. If you have had a bad day, take the time out to deal with it, so you don't affect the lives of others negatively. Your responsibility is to be a light in the darkness. Your community/circle of influence desperately needs you.

Talk Time

 Mother's Question: Why do you feel God has placed you in your community/circle of influence? What is one thing you can do to be a light for your community/circle of influence?

 Daughter's Question: Why do you feel God has placed you in your community/circle of influence? What is one thing you can do to be a light for your community/circle of influence?

Agreement: We (your signatures) _____ and _____ agree to look for opportunities to bless our community/circle of influence.

Prayer: Dear Heavenly Father, thank you for placing me here. Show me what your call is for me in this place. Amen.

Notes

_____

_____

_____

_____

_____

_____

_____

_____

_____

_____

_____

_____

_____

_____

_____

Communications

Let the wise listen and add to their learning, and
let the discerning get guidance

Proverbs 1:5 (NIV)

At the R2WW, one of the other tools we believe will help
you in the battle for your purity is to understand as much
as you can about communication. We are going to spend
the next few days going over some important tips. First,
let's start with the most important aspect of communication: listening.

We are all taught how to read, write and talk, but most
of us are not taught how to listen! Did you ever hear anyone say, "Today, we are going to learn how to listen"? I
certainly do not remember that. What I do remember
is people saying, "Sit down, be quiet, and listen." In my
mind, I always thought "How do I do that?" My mind
is always running at the speed of light with to-do lists,
thoughts of people I love, just someone passing by, or
maybe that paint on the wall that I do not like. How
about you?

We spend percentages of our average day:

- Writing9%
- Reading16%
- Speaking30%
- Listening45%

Writing	9%
Reading	16%
Speaking	30%
Listening	**45%**

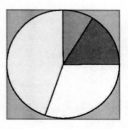

Because we are programmed to listen autobiographically, we tend to respond to what we hear in one of four ways. We evaluate—we either agree or disagree; we probe—we ask questions from our own frame of reference; we advise—we give counsel based on our own experience; or we interpret—we try to figure people out, to explain their motives, their behaviour, based on our own motives and behaviour.

God gave us two ears and one mouth for a reason: to listen more than we talk. We will talk more about listening skills over the next few days.

Why is it important to listen?

> He who talks knows his own information. But he, who listens, knows his and other's information.
>
> —Unknown

Talk Time

 Mother's Question: Did you ever learn how to listen? What do you struggle with most when it comes to listening?

 Daughter's Question: Honestly answer: do you really listen to your mom? Ask your mom the same: does she listen to you?

Agreement: We (your signatures) _____ and _____ agree to take time to learn more about how to improve our listening skills.

Prayer: Dear Heavenly Father, thank you for the ability to communicate. Show us your desire for our communications with others. Amen.

Notes

Communications Part 2

Be gracious in your speech. The goal is to bring out the best in others in a conversation, not put them down, and not cut them out.

Colossians 4:6 (MSG)

If only we could remember that communication is more than just words, I believe our relationships would be stronger, or at the least, we would be better understood!

Here are some tips from *Communicating Effectively for Dummies* by Marty Brounstein:

If you only hear my words, you won't understand my message.

A speaker's message contains three components:

- *Words:* The verbal component of the message; that is, what the speaker is saying.

- *Tone of voice:* The flavor that comes from your voice that impacts how the words are being said. Different from volume, which is how loud or soft you speak, tone involves the inflection being heard and the level of sincerity coming out of your voice.

- *Body language:* A nonverbal component that further describes how the speaker's message is being conveyed. Body language includes all the things you do with your body to express your message. This includes the use of gestures, eye contact, facial expressions, and posture.

Body language and tone of voice have great influence over the meaning of a speaker's message. To recognize their impact on the meaning of a message, try this out:

- Say the following sentence with a smile on your face: "Today is a beautiful day."

- Now repeat the same sentence with a frown on your face.

- What happened to your message from the first time to the second time it was said? When your facial expression changed, your message's meaning changed from a positive outlook to a negative one.

- Say the following sentence in a calm and sincere tone: "Today is a beautiful day."

- *Now repeat the same sentence with a sarcastic tone in your voice.*

- What happened to your message from the first to the second time it was said? When your tone of voice changed, your message's meaning changed from one of patient truthfulness to one of annoyed deceit.

If I would have you take away anything from this information, it is the importance of your tone. My granddaughter and I had a conversation just the other day on tone. At times, you won't even hear the tone you are speaking. She happened to say something, and her tone made it sound like she was demanding, not asking. We talked about it right after, and she had not even realized that she had asked her question in that manner.

I do want to give a check to you, Moms and Dads. Take a moment to look back at the homes you were raised in. What was the tone used? You may not even know what your tone is. If you have heard and expressed things in a harsh tone all your life, this would make it just normal to you. Ask your family and friends how you come across; this is a good life lesson.

Talk Time

Mother's Question: Having read this information does it make you think about how the other elements of communication may affect your conversations with your daughter?

Daughter's Question: Having read this information does it make you think about how the other elements of communication may affect your conversations with your mom?

Agreement: We (your signatures) _____ and _____ agree to become more aware of the other elements of communication with each other.

Prayer: Dear Heavenly Father, you are the greatest communicator of all times. Please show us how to be better at sharing our thoughts and feelings with others, so they can see our true heart. Amen.

Notes

Communications Part 3

Each of you should look not only to your own
interests, but also to the interests of others.

Philippians 2:4 (NIV)

Think about the last time you asked someone, "How are
you?" Do you recall waiting for a response or did you ask
something else or perhaps walked away before they could
answer? So many people ask, "How are you?" Then, not
only do we not listen to the reply, but those who are the
recipient of the question do not even register it as a real
question, and they reply with a simple "Fine," no matter
how they feel!

To help you understand the best form of listening,
I will share with you some information from Steven
Covey's book, *The 7 Habits of Highly Effective People*.

Empathic Listening

"Seek first to understand" involves a very deep
shift in paradigm. We typically seek first to be
understood. Most people do not listen with the
intent to understand; they listen with the intent
to reply. They're filtering everything through their
own paradigms, reading their autobiography into
other people's lives.

When another person speaks, we are usually listening at one of four levels. We may be ignoring another person, not really listening at all. We may practice pretending. "Yeah. Uh-huh. Right." We may practice selective listening, hearing only certain parts of the conversation. We often do this when we are listening to the constant chatter of a preschool child. Or we may even practice attentive listening, paying attention, and focusing energy on the words that are being said. But very few of us ever practice the fifth level, the highest form of listening, empathic listening.

When I say empathic listening, I mean listening with the intent to understand. I mean seeking first to understand, to really understand. It's an entirely different paradigm.

Empathic (from empathy) listening gets inside another person's frame of reference. You look out through it, you see the world the way they see the world, you understand their paradigm, and you understand how they feel.

Empathic listening involves much more than registering, reflecting, or even understanding the words that are said. Communications experts estimate, in fact, that only 10 percent of our communication is represented by the words we say. Another 30 percent is represented by our sounds and 60 percent by our body language. In empathic listening, you listen with your ears, but you also, and more importantly, listen with your heart. You listen for feeling and meaning. You listen for behaviour. You use your right brain as well as your left. You sense, you intuit, you feel.

Empathic listening is so powerful because it gives you accurate data to work with. Instead of projecting your own autobiography and assuming thoughts, feelings, motives, and interpretation, you are dealing with the reality inside another person's head and heart. You are listening to understand. You are focused on receiving the deep communication of another human soul.

Empathic listening is also risky. It takes a great deal of security to go into a deep listening experience because you open yourself up to be influenced. You become vulnerable. It's a paradox, in a sense, because in order to have influence, you have to be influenced. That means you have to really understand.

When teaching on communications, I use a visual that relates to empathic listening. I share that it is removing your filters when listening. Moms, this will be more related to you because you have more life experience that increases your filters. Filters are those experiences that jade our judgment. An example of this would be: you attended parties when you were younger and now believe that all parties are bad. The mention from your daughter of going to a party will create all kinds of images that will stop you from fully listening to her request.

Girls, I hate to tell you this, but you too have already created filters when listening to your mom. You will tend to believe the way she reacted before will be how she will always react. Sometimes her reactions are caused by her day, not by you, so try to set aside your fears to communicate.

Take what you have read today and evaluate your "empathic" listening skills, and see where you can make a conscious effort to be a better listener.

Talk Time

 Mother's Question: Tell your daughter how you think she listens to you. How would you like her to listen?

 Daughter's Question: Tell your mother how you think she listens to you. How would you like her to listen?

Agreement: We (your signatures) _____ and _____ agree to work on listening empathetically.

Prayer: Dear Heavenly Father, thank you for bringing us these lessons on listening. Help us to honestly listen to what others are saying, not what we think they are saying. Amen.

Communications Part 4

Listen, my sons, to a father's instruction; pay attention and gain understanding.

Proverbs 4:1 (NIV)

All your life, listening will be something you have to continuously work on. I have given you a few vital steps to improve your listening skills. Here are six more basic steps to help you further:

The Six Steps to Effective Listening

1. Concentrate—Make sure you hear the message (using both eyes and ears). Focus in on the person who is speaking, not what is going on around you, and remember to listen with not only your ears but your heart, too.

2. Acknowledge—Let the person know that you are listening. Use eye contact and verbal clues, like saying, "Yes," "Tell me more," and the best one for women, "How do you feel about that?"

3. Respond—Participate in the conversation. Use clarifying and directive questions.

4. Exercise emotional control—Do not make an immediate judgment on the message that you hear. This is where your filters will come in.

5. Sense—Women especially are known to have intuition (the act or faculty of knowing or sensing without the use of rational processes). Use this tool to communicate better.

6. Structure—Make sure to clarify what you hear and that you understand the true message being relayed.

One other area is really listening to advice that people who love you are giving. The next time your mom or dad wants to talk, think about the above steps to listening. Make an effort to truly hear what is being said. On the flip side of that, teen's parents should do the same.

Let me ask you this, have you heard God speak lately? These skills should also be applied to talking with our Heavenly Father. If we can't even listen to what others are saying, then how do we expect to listen to God?

Remember, God gave us two ears and one mouth; perhaps, that means we should use our ears twice as much.

Talk Time

 Mother's Question: When was the last time you had a conversation with God? How did it go?

 Daughter's Question: Have you ever heard God tell you something so clearly that you knew beyond a doubt that it was him?

Agreement: We (your signatures) _____ and _____ agree to take more time to hear what God has to say as well as those who love us.

Prayer: Dear Heavenly Father, help us to hear you more clearly. Amen.

Notes

_____

_____

_____

_____

_____

_____

_____

_____

_____

_____

_____

_____

_____

_____

_____

The Purity of Communications

The tongue has the power of life and death, and
those who love it will eat its fruit.

Proverbs 18:21 (NIV)

We will be looking further into the topic of communications through personality types and dealing with difficult situations and people later on in this devotional. But for today, I want to discuss with you the concept of purity in our communications.

The above scripture tells us that there is life and death in the power of the tongue. I have come to believe that words will hurt deeper and last longer than any physical injury we may receive. To heal the wounding of words may take a lifetime, while the body is made to heal itself rather quickly.

Reflecting back on some of the words spoken into my life, I can see where some were positive, but honestly there were more often than not negative words spoken. Until I was an adult and I discovered how those words were affecting my spiritual growth, my education, and my emotions, I allowed those negative words to control who I was. I know now beyond a shadow of a doubt that most of those words were not intentionally spoken with a desire to hurt me. People don't set out to hurt other people. Their past and current situation in life as well as not knowing God's truth of loving one another will cause them to hurt others through their words. To this day, many people are still unaware of the effects their words had on me. In light of this I have made an effort to watch the words I speak to everyone and especially those I love. I pray that God would heal any wounds my words may have caused others.

A couple of days from now, we are going to take a further look into curses and blessings. One of the days in this section will be related to spoken words. The information I have provided there is a great reminder that we truly need to think before we speak. Remember the old saying, "If you have nothing nice to say, don't say anything at all." This was my Grandma's favorite saying and even today, after she has passed I can honestly say she lived what she preached.

Just a note: correction and feedback are sometimes deemed as unkind words, but words spoken in love to help someone grow are to be welcomed. Ecclesiastes 7:5 says: "Better to be criticized by a wise person than to be praised by a fool." Look for wisdom in correction and before becoming defensive, see the heart of the person correcting. Then take it to the Lord and ask him what needs to be changed. Most of all, take only what is positive and uplifting, that which will produce a change towards a more godly life.

Talk Time

 Mother's Question: Share a time when you let the power of your tongue hurt your daughter, and use this time to repent and seek forgiveness.

 Daughter's Question: Share a time when you let the power of your tongue hurt your mother, and use this time to repent and seek forgiveness.

Agreement: We (your signatures) _____ and _____ agree to become mindful of what we say—that we lift others up and not tear them down.

Prayer: Dear Heavenly Father, show us where we have hurt people by what we have said and help us to make amends and ask for forgiveness. Help us to let go of our own pain by forgiving those who have hurt us by their words. Amen.

Notes

Understanding Personality Types

Always be humble and gentle. Be patient with each other, making allowance for each other's faults because of your love.

Ephesians 4:2 (NLT)

Saturday afternoon of the R2WW retreat, we take the moms and daughters through a personality test. We have used the True Colours model for the test. You can take this test free of charge on the True Colours site: www.truecolorstest.com/True_Colors_Test.shtml. If you are unable to do the test online, use these brief personality descriptions below to give you an idea of your personality type.

Just before we get started I would like to say something. God designed our personality types and you need to know that he is never limited, so there is much more depth to your personality than any test can ever measure. For example some people are introverts, extroverts, we each have our family history, and so much more that plays a part in who you are. Remember, this is just a glimpse to help you understand a little more about people and yourself.

GOLD	GREEN
• Decisive	• Orderly
• Independent	• Performs exacting work
• Tends to be dominant	• Likes controlled circumstances
• Strong willed	• Likes assurance of security
• Wants immediate results	• Uses critical thinking
• Causes action	• Follows rules
• Likes power and authority	• Read and follows instructions
• Likes freedom from control	• Prefers status quo
• Dislikes supervision	• Dislikes sudden or abrupt change
• Outspoken	• Tends to be serious and persistent
• Wants direct answers	• Cautious
• Restless	• Diplomatic
• Competitive	• Respectful
• Adventurous	• Agreeable
• Assertive	• Checks for accuracy
ORANGE	**BLUE**
• Optimistic	• Patient
• Tends to be exciting / stimulating	• Accommodating
• Generates enthusiasm	• Good listener
• Often dramatic	• Shows loyalty
• Talkative	• Concentrates on task accuracy
• Open and friendly	• Likes security and stability
• Likes working with people	• Needs good reason for change
• Likes participating in groups	• Home life a priority
• Desires to help others	• Expects credit for work done
• Wants freedom of expression	• Likes traditional procedures
• Wants for freedom from detail	• Dislikes conflict
• Likes change / spontaneity	• Neighbourly
• Persuasive	• Considerate towards others
• Appears confident	• Important to perform good work
• Likes recognition	• Pleasure in sharing and giving

Firstly, knowing your personality type is not an "Aha! This explains why I am like I am!" God made you as you are, but wants you to grow more like him in every way. As you read below, I want you to see that everyone is different. Not everything is supposed to be the way you want or the way the other person wants. My husband often says if we are both the same, one of us isn't needed.

Here is my summary of the individual traits for each of the four personality types. You will find there are always two predominant colours describing your personality.

Gold

This is my strongest personality type; scoring the highest number you can at a 20. I always say I am a 20-carat gold. Gold personality types love plans; no spontaneity for us. My calendar tends to be booked up a year in advance. Surprise me with a visit, and it will not go so well. The towels in my bathroom hang in an orderly fashion; please put them back that way. My house has to be clean and in order at all times.

I have a to-do list, and I am at my best when I can check everything off, although that never happens because I add to the bottom of every list. I always have a plan for the future and I live on a budget.

Orange

Now this personality type is my complete opposite. God has put them on this earth to help me be a better person. Oranges love spontaneity and love to have a good time. They are not organized—or should I say, they have their own system and it works best for them. They aren't stressed by the future, they live in today. They love to spend money and are usually in debt. They do not mind a mess because life is passing too fast to worry about housework.

Can you see why golds and oranges need each other so much? They help golds to relax and stop taking unimportant things, like housework, so seriously. Without golds, oranges would want to accomplish so many things but have a difficult time with structure to get things accomplished.

Blue

You will know a blue personality type; they are always waiting in line for a hug. They do not like conflict and will always try to avoid it. Blues are peacemakers and make everyone feel included. They love to buy gifts for people and to have social gatherings. Their door is always open. Go to a blue's at dinnertime, and they will just put on another plate and make you feel right at home. They are also awesome team players, every work environment or team sport needs a blue.

They tend to say sorry a lot, whether it is their fault or not; bump into a blue and they will apologize to you. They take the blame for a lot of things they don't even do, especially if it keeps the peace. They also tend to be a little indecisive only because they base their decisions on how everyone will feel about the outcome.

Green

And as you can imagine, the opposite of a blue personality type would be someone who reasons through logic rather than feelings. These are the great analyzers of our times; they are our deep thinkers, the academics. They like lots of information and want time to sort through it to make good decisions.

Green and blue personality types need each other to balance out. Where a blue will deal with all decisions on an emotional level, greens will add a logical pattern to the process. Greens have a tendency to separate from people, and a blue helps them to interact as they always include everyone. Greens have a bit of a harsh edge to them, and blues will help bring out the softer side.

God said he created us in his image and he encompasses all personality types. He asks us to be more like his Son, who spent his time on earth being all things to all people. So, let me ask you: if we are to be more Christlike, do we need to work at understanding and accepting each personality type as they are? Yes! Remember, God said we are all perfectly and wonderfully made; that means just the way you are and just as I am. Find the value in each person and together with your value you have so much more to offer.

Talk Time

Mother's Question: In reviewing the different personality types, what did you learn about your relationship with your daughter, remembering that God made her just the way she is?

Daughter's Question: In reviewing the different personality types, what did you learn about your relationship with your mother, remembering that God made her just the way she is?

Agreement: We (your signatures) _____ and _____ agree to appreciate our differences, to know God has planned for us to bring out the best in each other.

Prayer: Dear Heavenly Father, thank you for creating each and every one of us differently. Show us how to be a complement to others we love and know. Amen.

Dealing with Difficult People

> Make allowance for each other's faults, and forgive anyone who offends you. Remember, the Lord forgave you, so you must forgive others.
>
> Colossians 3:13–14 (NLT)

One of the best books I read on dealing with difficult people is *Coping with Difficult Situations* by Robert M. Bramson. It taught me that, just as we have different personality types, we also have different behaviours when dealing with conflict. In this book, they give numerous behaviour styles and tips on coping with each one individually. The list is too large to provide here, so please pick up the book; I can assure you, you will find it interesting.

Below you will find six common steps to deal with every style. This is from that same book.

Use These Six Steps to Deal with Any Behavioral Style

• Assess the situation.
• Stop wishing difficult people were different.

- Get some distance between you and the diffi-cult behaviour.

- Formulate a coping plan.

- Implement your plan.

- Monitor the effectiveness of your coping strat-egy, modifying it where appropriate.

Defensive Behaviour in Yourself and Others

In my opinion, the most common unhealthy behaviour when dealing with a difficult situation is being defensive. People react defensively to situations in which they feel threatened and/or under pressure. These feelings create anxiety which touches the core of who they are in the way of needs, wants, and values. An attack at this level pen-etrates into the source of feelings: the fear that we may be deprived of that which we cherish most.

We each have ways of defending ourselves against threats, but there are recognizable patterns:

- Self-blame defensive strategy – I know this is all my fault, but…

- Being distracted defensive strategy – Ignoring whatever is being said.

- Explanation defensive strategy – Giving reasons why it has happened, and making excuses for our words and actions.

These are a few defensive strategies. Although there are others, most can fit into these categories.

In coping with others' defensive behaviour, the more you avoid inadvertently threatening others, the less you will have to cope with their defensive and difficult behaviour.

In managing your own defensive mode, you must learn what you are like. Keep an eye on yourself. You'll be able to note when you are defensive. Pay attention to how you behave, what you say, and how you feel. Learn to freeze your behaviour the moment you recognize you are in defensive mode. If possible, take a short breath, try to find the threat, watch for reactions of defensiveness. This can help you to learn what triggers the behaviour.

Remember, in most cases, none of us are immediately aware of how we react and the impact we have on others. While we may not always be responsible for our reactions, we are responsible for how we react to our reactions. Always ask for forgiveness when you have acted inappropriately. If you think you have not acted inappropriately, ask yourself what you could have done differently, or where did that reaction come from? I think you will find the need for seeking forgiveness.

Talk Time

 Mother's Question: How do you handle difficult people, and how do you think you could improve your behaviour? Is there a current situation that, perhaps talking it out with your daughter, may create a much better outcome?

Daughter's Question: Same as Mom: How do you handle difficult people, and how do you think you could improve your behaviour? Is there a current situation that, perhaps by talking it out with your mom, may create a much better outcome?

Agreement: We (your signatures) _____ and _____ agree to try to stop and analyse situations before we react.

Prayer: Dear Heavenly Father, thank you for teaching us how to show grace in dealing with difficult situations. Amen.

Perceptions

Then make me truly happy by agreeing whole-
heartedly with each other, loving one another, and
working together with one mind and purpose. Do
not be selfish; do not try to impress others.

Philippians 2:2–3 (NLT)

In mature communications, it is understood that there
are three truths: mine, yours, and then the ultimate
truth—God's. We tend to live in a world where we communicate through our perceptions. We believe what we
think is right. There is no one that is completely right
about everything. We interpret what is truth through our
past experiences and limited understandings.

An example of this is might be:

Mom, your daughter has asked to hang out at the
mall, and from your previous experience, perhaps a comment from a friend, or maybe even something you have
heard on the news, you believe it is the most unsafe place
for your daughter. You have forgotten to taken the time
to ask your daughter what her plans really are and who
she is going with. Your perceptions have you already setting rules and boundaries that may not even be necessary.

If you were to take a moment and block these negative thoughts and ask some important questions, you may
find out she is going with friends you really trust. They

have a plan of where they are going to hang out and you are actually okay with that spot. Ah, but, daughter, this is not only something your mom does. Say your mom has reacted this way before when you asked her to go to the mall. You will already be in defense mode; you may even be hiding things from her or demanding your way.

How do we learn to have mature conversations? It's about full disclosure of information and also knowing that what you're saying is only from your perspective. Be more open-minded, pray for wisdom, and ask open-ended questions.

Same conversation about the mall, but your daughter has spent time in prayer, asking God if this is what she should do, and if he would confirm that through you. Start with, "Mom, would you mind if I go to the mall tonight. I am going with so-and-so, and we will be at such-and-such place. What time would you like me home?" If you think it is too early for your liking, ask if there is something she needs you to do, and if that is why she is asking you to be home at that time. If not, then ask, "Why is it important for me to be home at that time?" Hear her out, and live with it; create trust by being home on time or even a little earlier. Mom, do not forget to be flexible and look at it through your daughter's eyes. Also, take time to pray and ask God what he thinks of the situation. Always remember, you are raising adults, not children; they need to safely make their own choices. Guide, not tell them how to set their direction.

Remember, one person's perception equals one person's reality, and only God knows the total truth and sees into the future. Go to him in prayer to seek the truth.

Talk Time

Mother's Question: Where can you see that your perception gets in the way of making good decisions?

Daughter's Question: Can you see where perception gets in the way of making a good decision? When is a time you haven't seen things from your mom's point of view?

Agreement: We (your signatures) _____ and _____ agree to remember there are always three truths: mine, yours, and God's. Pray, ask him for help in your communications. Ask him to show you when your perceptions are getting in the way.

Prayer: Dear Heavenly Father, help us to search you and to understand—not through our own perceptions—but to see your truth. Amen.

Notes

_____

_____

_____

_____

_____

_____

_____

_____

_____

_____

_____

_____

_____

_____

Motives of the Heart

The purpose of my instruction is that all believers
would be filled with love that comes from a pure
heart, a clear conscience, and genuine faith.

1 Timothy 1:5 (NLT)

Check Engine Light,
Check Motive Light

In a vehicle, the check engine light tells us something is
wrong, and if it goes off and is not looked after in a timely
manner, your motor will seize up. So let's use that same
analogy of the check engine light on our motives.

What if every time there was something wrong with
our motives, God would flash a red "Check Motive" light
for all to see? Would we be willing to let others see it and
find a way to fix it? Who would be our mechanic?

We are judged by our motives. The Bible says God
looks at our heart and he sees what a good motive is or
what is not.

I'll give you an example from my life. I have a heart to
give; I'm not so good when it comes to receiving. There is
part of me that feels unworthy to receive. I got to a point
in my life where giving was all I did. Once I was giving
from that point, I can guarantee you I was no longer giv-

ing from a place of love. I gave to be loved. That's where the act of giving has to come from God's desires. He wants a joyful and generous giver—a giver who gives to love not be loved; we cannot always do that on our own, we need his help.

When I was at the point of exhaustion and could not give anymore, I started to feel that no one loved me. Feeling unloved, I was driven into the arms of God where I found his refreshing love. He gently showed me how he had allowed me to be brought to this place of feeling unloved. He then showed me the motive that I continually gave from; it was to have people like me and need me, and even love me, "he showed me that this was not his desire."

It was a struggle to unlearn this behaviuor (and still at times I go back to giving to be loved), but through this I learned that I am precious because he created me. Even if people do not always like me, he will always love me.

My advice: Look at where your motives come from. Do a heart check and always renew your mind in the Lord to ensure your motives are right. Who better to have as our mechanic than the one who made us?

Talk Time

 Mother's Question: Can you see where your motives could be off and need a tune up?

 Daughter's Question: Same as Mom: Can you see where your motives could be off and need a tune up?

Agreement: We (your signatures) _____ and _____ agree to check our motives on a regular basis and give them a tune-up when needed.

Prayer: Dear Heavenly Father, show us where our motives are off, direct our steps, show us any hidden motives. Help us to correct them and bring them back in line with your will. Amen.

Notes

_____

_____

_____

_____

_____

_____

_____

_____

_____

_____

_____

_____

_____

_____

_____

_____

Facts vs. Feelings

> Therefore, as God's chosen people, holy and dearly loved, clothe yourselves with compassion, kindness, humility, gentleness and patience.
>
> Colossians 3:12 (NIV)

Communicating in only the facts will leave a relationship dead. We are humans and are made up of feelings and logic. It is hard in the rush of today's society to communicate all the facts, let alone spend the time and energy on diving into feelings.

I have made it a point to try to have effective communication with the ones I love. That means when I ask how their day was, "Fine" is not an answer I choose to acknowledge. This is a fact-level answer, whether it is true or not.

What are facts? They are pieces of information about circumstances that exist or events that have occurred, "Like collecting all the legal facts for a case going to court."

What are feelings? They are experiences of affective and emotional states, such as, "She is feeling sad and lonely."

Mom, I know what it is like to have discussions with your kids. You say to your daughter, "How was your day?" and I bet 90 percent of the time, her response has been,

"Fine." I can also guess your answer: "Oh, that's good." It takes energy and time to get to feelings. But, if we truly ever want to intimately know the ones we love, we must get to the feelings in our communications.

Where do we start? My answer would be conversations with open-ended questions. Do not just ask how their day was. Ask, "Whom did you hang out with today?" "Did you go anywhere or just hang around the school yard?" "Who do you spend a lot of time with?" Now you have a conversation going. Or maybe not. If she is like my granddaughter, she would say, "Can we listen to Odyssey now?" My reply to her always is, "Can we talk for five more minutes first? I really care about what happened in your day."

Once you have her talking, ask how certain things make her feel. What does it feel like when you hang out with that person? If she says, "I don't know," give her feeling examples. "Does it make you happy or calm?"

You are a safe place for your daughter to start to learn to express her feelings. If you have boys, this is such an important part of their upbringing. They will need to be able to discuss their feelings with their wives and families, and for men, this is not natural. And girls, help your brothers talk about feelings and take time to pray for the man you will marry, that he is taught how to share his feelings too.

Remember also that facts are important, but how you feel about those facts makes life come alive.

Talk Time

 Mother's Question: What feelings do you find hard to express and why?

 Daughter's Question: Can you express feelings or is it hard to do?

Agreement: We (your signatures) _____ and _____ agree to try to communicate below the surface level and to talk about our feelings.

Prayer: Dear Heavenly Father, show us how to appropriately express and share our feelings and then how to not let them take control of our lives. Amen.

Notes

_____

_____

_____

_____

_____

_____

_____

_____

_____

_____

_____

_____

_____

_____

_____

_____

Expectation vs. Gratitude

And give thanks for everything to God the Father
in the name of our Lord Jesus Christ.

Ephesians 5:20 (NLT)

Girls, I am going to start this conversation speaking to
you. May I ask you a question? When was the last time
you did something special for your mom (without being
asked)? Not a chore that is expected; maybe something
like, when your mom is in the shower, you go make her
bed and perhaps put a chocolate on her pillow.

In close, loving relationships, we come to expect things.
Things like my mom is supposed to cook, clean do the
laundry, and my daughter is supposed to clean her room,
do her homework, not date until we her parents are ready
for it, and so on. Subsequently, gratitude for things we do
gets thrown out the window.

Let's look for a minute, Mom, at something you can
perhaps relate. When you got engaged, automatically, you
started to create a list of expectations. Such as, when we
get married, we will live in this kind of house, have this
many kids, he will work, I will stay home. Even, we will
both go to bed at the very same time and cuddle, and so
on. The day after your honeymoon, you already start to
realize that not all those dreams (expectations) you had
are going to come true, or perhaps they are going to come

later than you expected. So now, the choice is to see your husband through the eyes of your expectations or but to see him through the eyes of gratitude. Finding those things he does well and being thankful for them.

A word of wisdom to daughters, never use someone else's parents to set the expectation for yours. Be thankful for what you have; there are children without a home, food, or parents. You are truly blessed. See your parents through eyes of gratitude.

Mom, the same goes for you. When was the last time you did something extra special for your daughter? On Valentine's Day, I used to take Laura a rose and a stuffy to her school, and then I would have them call her to the office to receive her special gift (and of course, I would have left already). It was important to me to show my gratitude for her being in my life.

If we release all our relational expectations to God (as he is the only one who can meet all our needs) it will allow us to value what people do for us and not to just expect that they should have to do it.

Talk Time

 Mother's Question: Have you looked through the eyes of thankfulness for your daughter?

 Daughter's Question: Have you looked through the eyes of thankfulness for your mom?

Agreement: We (your signatures) _____ and _____ agree to make a conscious effort to be thankful for the gift of our family. Not to look at them for what they can do for us. To show them we are thankful to have them in our lives.

Prayer: Dear Heavenly Father, show us ways to show the ones we love how special they are and how much we love them. Amen.

Notes

Rules for Fighting Fair

> Instead, we will speak the truth in love, growing in every way more and more like Christ, who is the head of his body, the church.
>
> Ephesians 4:15 (NLT)

Rules for fighting fair, impossible! Fights happen in the heat of the moment, so how do we expect to follow any rules? It is about being proactive not reactive, plan to fight and then create a plan for a successful outcome.

Listen with the intent to understand (yes, I've said it before, and yes, it is still important). Let your teens know that you heard them and understood them, even when the decision must remain the same. Show compassion and sympathy by using phrases such as: "I know it is tough, I know you are disappointed, and even so, or nevertheless, you cannot use the car tonight."

Distinguish between privileges and rights. Some of the rights teens should expect are a warm shelter, clothing, love, food, educational opportunities, and safety. Many of the other things they expect, such as designer clothing, telephones, computers, movie money, etc., are not rights—they are privileges. Sal Severe, author of *How to Behave So Your Children Will Too*, advises parents not to "give the ice cream away for free." When privileges are tied to appropriate behaviour, kids have more motivation to behave appropriately.

Asking open-ended questions that begin with how, when, where, who, or what is a great place to start. Tensions ease and the shift to problem-solving comes naturally. A great resource describing in more detail how to apply this is the book *I Do Not Have to Make Everything All Better* by Gary and Joy Lundberg.

Not all conflicts are resolved easily. Tougher situations require a mechanism that keeps underlying emotional tension in control. Together, decide how to handle future conflict. If you can keep in mind some of these helpful hints for fighting fair you will have a better chance at a resolution or at least a rational exchange:

- Issues from the past will stay in the past.

- Honesty between parties will be maintained.

- All parties agree that everyone needs to be informed.

- Issues will be discussed in a calm manner. Should conversations become heated, both parties agree to physically separate.

- Parents and teens list and prioritize areas of conflict to be addressed for each area.

- Each party explains the situation from their point of view.

- Parents and teens together develop a solution that is workable for all.

- Record agreements reached and then prepare a written agreement that parents and teens must sign. This agreement needs to be accessible so you can refer to it when behavior doesn't change.

- When intense fellowship (my favorite name for referring to fighting) does occur these are the absolute no, no's:

  No name calling

  No swearing

  No saying hurtful things

  No interrupting

- When it comes to discipline make sure what is given fits the situation. It may be wise to ask your child to have input into the disciplines set. If you request them to reverse roles, thinking as a parent, you may find they are harder on themselves.

- Remember always to pick wisely the mountains you want to die on. If you ask yourself "will this behavior affect her safety, health, reputation or character," or will this issue matter in 5 years. Do this and you will see what is worth fighting for.

Remember that God created conflict and he also created a way to resolve it. The best place to start is with prayer and then to recognize what you have done to add to this heated conversation. The Scriptures say, "Take the plank from your eye before you try to remove the speck from someone else." Translated, it means you need to look at your own faults before you try to change others.

Talk Time

 Mother's Question: What type of conflict resolution happened in your childhood home? What worked and what did not?

 Daughter's Question: Where do you see that you need to improve your conflict skills?

Agreement: We (your signatures) _____ and _____ agree to follow the fair fighting rules.

Prayer: Dear Heavenly Father, you allow for conflict to help us grow; let us always look to learn and change. Amen.

Living with our Consequences

I know how bad I've been; my sins are staring me down. You're the One I've violated, and you've seen it all, seen the full extent of my evil. You have all the facts before you; whatever you decide about me is fair.

Psalm 51:3–4 (MSG)

I have witnessed many times Christians who throw their hands up and say, "God, why me?" I sometimes feel like saying, "Why not you?" And, "Are you sure that what is happening is not something you have played a part in?"

I have spent a lot of time thinking about my past failures. In all cases, my actions may not have always created all the problems, but certainly, they always had some effect on the outcome.

You will hear a lot of people say not to live in your past, and believe me, they are right. Don't *live* there, but *look* there for the changes that can be made today.

We need to take responsibility for our actions; it is human nature for us to place blame. It is difficult to admit when we have failed, but I challenge you to look at your failures in a positive light. I once heard a pastor's sermon that said, "In order to succeed, failure is necessary." When Thomas Edison was asked about his 2,000 failures in making the light bulb, he said that he had not failed, but he had successfully identified 2,000 ways not to make a light bulb. I always say a mistake is never a mistake—it is a lesson to create change.

Own your faults, then ask for forgiveness and then repent. Remember, repenting is different than apologizing; repenting means making a genuine effort to change the behaviour.

Wouldn't it be great if we could freeze-frame all our actions and then come outside of ourselves to analyze them, to see what the results of those actions will create in the future? I can testify that my actions never only affected me. They always affected others and, perhaps, even people I will never know. I have watched my son's life. When I see where he struggles in areas of his life, 80 percent of the time, I can see where my actions as a parent laid the foundation for his struggle.

Girls, do not mistake this to be an adult issue only, your own actions and words have power that alter the future.

During our formative years, we tend to live in the here and now; in saying that, I wonder if perhaps in today's culture some adults do that as well. As parents, we are so busy we have no time to think about tomorrow. If we could all slow down long enough to freeze frame our important decisions and evaluate the future consequences, we might take the time to pray for God's assistance and to seek wise godly council. Could you imagine the changes that would happen in ourselves, our families, and the future generations if we slowed down long enough to think through consequences before taking action?

Talk Time

Mother's Question: Talk about an action you took that has created a consequence you struggle with now.

Daughter's Question: What are some things you have done that you wish you hadn't?

Agreement: We (your signatures) _____ and _____ agree to take responsibility for our actions. We accept the fact that we may fail, but realize there is always forgiveness.

Prayer: Dear Heavenly Father, help us to have grace for ourselves and others. Help us to ask forgiveness and seek repentance. Show us what we can do to change our actions and words so the consequences do not affect others negatively. Amen.

Notes

Love Tank Runs Better on Full

So encourage each other and build each other up,
just as you are already doing.

1 Thessalonians 5:11 (NLT)

I once heard someone say, "People do not care how much you know until they know how much you care." Think of it this way, if you open an investment account and you put nothing in the account, you have no interest. Invest time and effort into your relationships and you might see some interest in what you have to say. Likewise if a gas tank in a car isn't full, it won't run. Neither will you run on an empty love tank.

"Ah," you ask, "how do you invest to create interest–or fill someone's love tank?"

Look for (or create) opportunities to spend meaningful time together. Offer specific feedback and praise when your teen meets your behavioural expectations. Let your teen know what you like about him/her; avoid down-talking, belittling, or humiliating your daughter. Remember to praise in public and correct in private.

Teens have less motivation to behave in ways that please parents when the parent/teen relationship is strained. Think of yourself: if your boss is on your case more often than not, do you feel like doing anything to please him/her? I know I don't.

My husband and I have often looked back at our parenting years, and it is easy now to see the mistakes (remember, there are no perfect parents) we made. I heard one lady say, "Children should be born with an instruction manual." What do I say to that? "There is! It is called the Bible, our Book of Instructions before Leaving Earth." But if you are like me, nobody showed me how to use the Bible as a manual for life. Now though, if I want a scripture-based answer, I look in the concordance or ask my pastor.

One thing my husband and I often admit to and speak about at the R2WW is how when we were in the thick of parenting, our tendency was to see the 10 percent our kids did wrong and want to correct them. We missed the 90 percent they did right! Take the time every day to find something your kids have done right and *tell them*!

The first night of the R2WW retreat, before the girls are sent to their rooms for the night, I sneak in to the girls PJ party and I read them a bedtime story called "The Wimmicks." I ask the girls if their moms read them bedtime stories. They say sadly, "No." Whenever my granddaughter spends the night, she always waits in anticipation for our story time. It is not only time for our story, but this is the time of day when she has my total attention. And of course, she does not want to sleep, so it is the best time to ask her any questions. She will actually talk to me because she does not want the day to end. Find a time with your kids when they are apt to really talk to you; you will be surprised at the conversations you may never have had otherwise.

Okay, girls, this is not all about you and your tank. When is the last time you filled your mom's love tank? She needs you to help fill her up as she is always giving to her family. Have you complimented her lately, asked her what you could help with, done something without being asked? No one can run on an empty love tank—at least not for long!

Talk Time

 Mother's Question: How is your love tank, Mom? Are you running on empty? What can your daughter do to help?

 Daughter's Question: How is your love tank? Are you running on empty? What can your mom do to help?

Agreement: We (your signatures) _____ and _____ agree to be intentional in keeping each other feeling loved.

Prayer: Dear Heavenly Father, thank you for the mom/ daughter you have given me. Help me to find ways to show her how much I love and appreciate her. Amen.

Notes

Honesty and Trust

> Instead, we will speak the truth in love, growing in every way more and more like Christ, who is the head of his body, the church.
>
> Ephesians 4:15–16 (NLT)

At our R2WW retreats, we always have a mom and daughter share a short talk on an experience they had where building honesty and trust into their relationship was difficult.

You would think being honest is so easy, but it is not. Remember the old saying "Oh what wicked ways we weave when we practice to deceive." Sure, we always have a desire to tell the truth, but it so easy to exaggerate or shade the truth just a bit. What about not saying anything because what they do not know cannot hurt them, or changing the truth just a bit, so we look like the better person? It becomes a slippery slope and climbing back up is sure harder than sliding down. After telling lies for an extended period of time those lies start to become your truth and in turn the truth may never be shared. The devil can give us all kinds of reasons to lie, but we need to fight against that temptation and we can only do that by asking God to help us.

There is a huge correlation between honesty and trust. What I value most in another person is that I can trust them. I also want them to know I will stand behind my word, but what if my word has been tainted with dishonesty? The trust tends to fade, and it is always work to regain it.

An example of where trust is tested: you ask your mom if you can go to a party. You tell her the parents are going to be there, there will be no wrong conduct, there are lots of people she knows attending, and you will be home by 10:00 p.m.

This is all a lie; you come home after 12:00 a.m., drunk. Your mom finds out there were no parents and she knew no one there except the friend you went with.

May I tell you this—99 percent of the time trust is a gift you receive free of charge; you don't initially have to earn it. But throw it away by telling a lie, a half truth, or saying nothing, and then try to earn it back. It is almost impossible. Only time, effort and prayer can restore trust.

Scenario two from the story above: all you told your mom was true. Next time you want to go out, her answer will be guided by your honesty. Moms, remember your children will learn most of how to tell the truth by what you model.

Your reputation depends on your honesty. People want to trust you; give them a reason to.

Talk Time

 Mother's Question: Tell about a time when you were growing up and faced similar scenarios described above? Yes, both, when you told the truth and didn't!

Daughter's Question: Have you had a friend who has broken your trust by lying, and if so, how did you feel and react?

Agreement: We (your signatures) _____ and _____ agree to work at always being honest, and when we fail, to repent and ask God's help to always tell each other the truth.

Prayer: Dear Heavenly Father, thank you that you will be with us as we journey and learn how to always tell the truth. Amen.

Notes

The Danger of Gossip

The words of a gossip are like choice morsels;
they go down to a man's inmost parts.

Proverbs 18:8 (NIV)

Unfortunately, gossip tends to wrap its ugly tentacles around the lives of unsuspecting people. The biggest problem with it is that most people do not even realize when gossip is entering a conversation. Even worse is that they do not realize the impact gossip has. Gossip's rawest form is when something is said about one person to another, and they are not there to hear what is being said. It does not necessarily have to be saying something negative; it could be sharing someone's secrets or just talking about a person that is not there. With the birth of social media, there is a whole new danger in gossip—a comment made about someone on social network sites can now go viral; 1,000 if not 100,000 people will read what is being said.

I honestly admit that at times gossip tends to be a problem for me, as it is for everyone. You would think that as we get older, we would have learnt to correct these behaviours, but I firmly believe learning is a life-long journey.

God has been kind to show me the results of when I had been involved in a gossiping situation. He did this to help me see what the consequences of my actions were and so I could change and ask others for forgiveness.

Two of the situations he allowed me to see—that helped me to see the damage caused by gossip:

First scene he shared with me: I had just met someone, and on our first meeting, I was very judgmental towards them. It was not because of something they did, said, or even their mannerisms. God showed me it was my feelings and thoughts towards them. These were caused by something I had been told about them by someone else. They never even had a chance. With their first impression the gossip that had been shared with me created an untrue perception of who they were. Once I realized this, I tried very hard to erase what had been said, and to see them for the wonderful creation God had made. It took some time, but I can report that we are now friends and this person is amazing, truly amazing. I would tell you their name but, that would be gossiping.

Second scene he shared with me: I myself had been speaking about someone's shortcomings to a trusted friend. God showed me that not only was I damaging the person's character that I spoke of, but also my own. In sharing what I had with my friend it would lead her to believe that if I spoke behind this person's back, perhaps I would not hesitate talking about her.

Here are some additional dangers of gossip:

- Stressful feelings for those involved.
- Hurt feelings all around.
- Destruction of friendships and families.

- Destruction of the desire for people to share any personal things.

- Preventing communication that requires trust.

- Creating undeserved reputations for the people we speak about.

The following are a few helpful tips to use to stay away from or stop gossip:

1. Ignore it:
   - Stay away from people who gossip.
   - Simply leave the room or conversation when gossip starts.
   - Do not respond to gossip.
   - Ignore gossip.

2. Prevent it:
   - Don't start any of your own gossip.
   - Be a quick change artist—change the topic whenever a conversation leads into gossip.
   - Refuse to listen or respond to any gossip.
   - Hide your responses to gossip; don't show any hurt feelings or dramatic reactions to gossip.

3. Confront it:
   - Politely say, "I would rather we talk about that person when they are present."
   - Confront someone who is gossiping about you immediately. Calmly tell them you don't appreciate them talking about you.

- Stand up and say, "Would you like to have someone share that about you?" Don't wait around for the answer.

- Say that you do not talk about others unless it is positive.

I recently heard a speaker say to respond to gossip in this manner. "If you have not talked to your brother then why are you talking to me, and if you have talked to your brother, then why are you talking to me."

Talk Time

 Mother's Question: Have you been involved in gossip? Where has it gotten you?

 Daughter's Question: Do you gossip with your friends? Do you wish you could stop?

Agreement: We (your signatures) _____ and _____ agree to repent from previous bouts of gossip. We will avoid places and people where gossip happens.

Prayer: Dear Heavenly Father, help us to stay away from gossip. Help us always to allow people to show us themselves through your eyes, not the eyes of gossip. Amen.

Blessings

In you all the families of the earth shall be blessed.

Genesis 12:3 (nkjv)

The Saturday night of the R2WW we have a beautiful gala ball. We decorate the hall as if it were for a wedding. All the moms and daughters are in their finery. We have a wonderful four-course meal. But, if you were to ask me what the best part of that evening was, I would say, hands down, the time of blessing for the daughters. My husband and I came across the teaching of blessing ceremonies at a NAME Canada marriage conference. Some of the information I am about to share with you comes from the book *Bar Barakah: A Parent's Guide to a Christian Bar Mitzvah* by Craig Hill. Craig was the speaker at that marriage conference.

What Value Does a Blessing Have?

- Blessing is to empower to prosper.
- Being able to leave and cleave in marriage is directly tied to blessing. Where we have been blessed in an area, we are free to leave. Where we are not blessed, we are still bound to that parent. In Genesis 2:24, "For this cause a man shall leave

his father and mother and cleave to his wife and they will become one flesh."

- Blessing is God's method of imparting identity and blessing to the heart of a son or daughter. Imparting the truth of why they are here, and who they are.

- God separates identity from behaviour. We can honor the person without accepting the behaviour. Hate sin but honor the person. Forgiveness allows us to honor the person without accepting the behaviour.

Cursing is Satan's method of imparting identity and cursing into the heart of a son or daughter. Imparting a lie about who they are and why they are here.

Two primary things that cursing produces in a son or daughter:

- Judgment: cutting off the parent. You wounded me, I do not need you.

- An internal longing to get a blessing from the parent, trying and trying to finally have them say, "I'm proud of you."

A daughter who is not blessed by her father will judge him and cut herself off from him, after which the following list of outcomes may occur.

- Puts a shell around herself and is not predisposed to receive love from a man, which makes marriage difficult.

- Expects to be rejected by men.

- Identity established in self—work, achievement, femininity.

- May become supermom—any role she can excel in.

- Can become a strong leader for all the wrong reasons.

- Conflicts male authority's, she may prefer to work for a woman.

- Harsh in relationships, reproduces in herself or in her husband what she despised in her father.

- May not appear to be very feminine.

Tries to win her father's approval.

- Tries to win approval of men.

- Cares too much what others think.

- Emotional black hole, craving love no matter how much she gets.

- Undue striving for acceptance by men, whatever it takes.

- May be flirtatious or promiscuous in early years.

- Feelings more highly developed than logic— dumb blonde.

- When rejection by her father occurs, she may not develop male logic: map reading, or the ability to balance a checkbook.

- May appear stupid, but is highly intelligent.

- Highly self-critical, low self-confidence.

A daughter not blessed by her mother will judge her and cut herself off from her.

- Expects to be rejected by women.
- Identity in self—career, supermom.
- Attitude of "I do not need anyone else."
- Insensitive to the needs of others.
- Reproduces in her own life the qualities she despised in her mother.

Tries to win her mother's approval at all costs.

- Strives after love and acceptance, especially from women.
- Identity established in what other women think of her.
- May be very active in numbers of Bible studies and activities to the neglect of her husband.
- May despise her own femininity.

Over the next few days, we will look at the elements of a powerful blessing, but for today, "I want to set the stage."

The act of blessing should be done in public, although privately speaking words of encouragement to your children on a daily basis is so important.

In the Jewish custom where this idea of blessings comes from, the parents, on a regular basis, I believe usually Friday evenings during their meal time, would perform something similar to a ceremony. They would have a beautiful meal along with many customs and traditions;

during this time, they would bless each of their children publicly.

If you were to look at the success rate of the Jewish population, you would see that their success is intertwined with this time of being blessed. You can't help but succeed when someone is constantly speaking that over you.

Now we have the stage tomorrow, we will begin to look at the elements which make up a time of blessing.

To read more about blessing and to purchase other material or receive further training, see http://www.familyfoundations.com.

Talk Time

 Mother's Question: Did you receive blessings from your parents? How do you think that impacted your life?

 Daughter's Question: Do you feel your mom or dad has blessed you? Do you wish they would?

Agreement: We (your signatures) _____ and _____ agree to be conduits of blessing for our family. To strive to bless all who we come in contact with for we may be the only person who blesses them.

Prayer: Dear Heavenly Father, show us how to give blessings and help us retract curses by asking forgiveness of those we have cursed wherever possible. Amen.

Notes

Blessing:
The Element of Touch

Come near now and kiss me, my son.

Genesis 27:26 (NKJV)

Over the next few days, we will look at the elements that make up an unforgettable blessing. *The Blessing* by Gary Smalley and John Trent is our resource for what you are about to read.

In the Old Testament, the element of touch was an essential part of blessing your children. You can see in Genesis 27:11–12 that Jacob and Esau's father touched them when they were being blessed. I don't believe it stops in the Old Testament. In the New Testament, do you recall the story of the woman who was bleeding and only touched the hem of the robe of Jesus and was healed (healing is a blessing).

Not only at the time of blessing your children, but throughout their lives, touch is essential.

It has been reported that in orphanages where there was not enough staff to provide newborns with human touch, the children tended to suffer greatly and some in turn would die a premature death. It has also been clinically proven that girls who don't receive appropriate touch from their parents will look for it from other sources, more than likely male. Even more so, as girls grow up, their dads will find it awkward to touch their daughters, but it is so important that they receive appropriate hugs and kisses from their dads to negate their search for touch elsewhere.

As their parents, it is your responsibility to ensure that a healthy element of touch stays in your relationship. Make a conscious effort to find times that an appropriate touch, hug, or snuggle can be given. Don't look to force it or show public affection, perhaps, it is just a touch of the shoulder or a pat on their hand.

At our retreats, after all the ladies have received their makeovers, we have the moms and daughters go back to their rooms where they do each other's hair. We do this to bring touch back into their relationships. As your daughter hits about grade four, she no longer wants that hug from mom. When you drop her off at school and her friends are there, she will shy away from any physical intimacy. The touches you once had now becomes far and few between (except if they are blue personality type). Even the opportunity to brush her hair is seldom and possibly never. Moms, don't give up; she needs your affection as much as she needs her dad's.

When it comes to giving a blessing, the element of touch will bring it to the next level. When you are ready to bless your daughter, all it takes is for you to take her hand in yours, and then look into her eyes as you speak into her life with blessing. Incorporating this element will allow her not only to hear your blessing, but she will feel what you say, as well.

Don't fret; this may seems like a lot of preparation and learning for this time of blessing, but as it comes together, it will naturally just flow on that special occasion. Rely on the Holy Spirit; whatever you need to bless your children he will provide.

I know your daughters are reading this with you and perhaps they are getting a bit uncomfortable at the thought of the approaching event. Girls, I promise you this will be one of the highlights of your life. I pray that it becomes a family tradition and that your families are blessed often and that this legacy lives on after we are gone.

Talk Time

 Mother's Question: Talk to your daughter about a time when you felt the strong desire for touch (perhaps a hug), and if you didn't receive it, how that felt. Were your parents affectionate (in appropriate ways)?

 Daughter's Question: Talk to your mom about how it feels when you don't get the hugs or snuggles you need from her.

Agreement: We (your signatures) _____ and _____ agree to incorporate appropriate touch into our daily lives, and we will give each other hugs on a regular basis.

Prayer: Dear Heavenly Father, thank you for creating touch. Help us to touch people in (in appropriate ways) so they feel loved and connected.

Notes

_____

_____

_____

_____

_____

_____

_____

_____

_____

_____

_____

_____

_____

_____

_____

_____

Blessing: the Element of the Spoken Word

So speak encouraging words to one another. Build up hope so you'll all be together in this, no one left out, no one left behind.

1 Thessalonians 5:11 (MSG)

How many times growing up did you wish you had heard, "Good job! I am so proud of you!" or "We are so thankful you are in our home"?

In today's world of high stress and fast-paced living, speaking encouragement into our kids' lives is harder than ever to do. Who has time? Get the kids home, feed them, homework, housework, to bed, make lunches, and not only that, we are a taxi, running our kids to every event. After all this we are now supposed to remember to say something encouraging. Unfortunately, what we lack most is communication in our families. Busyness sucks our spirits dry causing us to want to just hide away. Great relationships take your energy and time.

Don't feel guilty; we all suffer from the busy syndrome. Not until I became a grandma did I learn to let go of the little things and focus on my granddaughter. Finally, at my age, I am less worried about success and chores and will do something with my granddaughter before any-thing else. I wish I would have done that with my son.

I can now see how much I missed out on having times of enjoyment with my son, times where I could have spo-ken words of encouragement into his life. And it is now too late for those special times; he is busy with a family of his own, work, and all those commitments that come along with life as an adult.

Had I known then what I know now, I would have spent time focusing on all the good things he did and not work so hard in correction mode. Of course, we need to bring our kids up right, but because of that we tend to use correction as the majority of our communications. Even if our kids are doing 90 percent right, we seem to focus on what needs to be corrected and forget the rest. I would have worried about that less and spent more time having fun, playing games, and having meaningful conversations with my son. In turn, I wouldn't have the regrets I do now.

Our words are so important to our children maturing into well-rounded adults. This is where the spoken word comes into our blessing. It is clinically proven that chil-dren who receive blessings from their parents won't feel the need to be overachievers in life and will have a high level of self-confidence. Later in life, they will have better marriages and create better family dynamics as they will know firsthand the necessity to bless others.

Take the time no matter how busy you are to regu-larly speak words of encouragement to your children— the rewards will be amazing. The words you speak will go on for generations to come. Leave a legacy of blessing, not cursing!

Talk Time

Mother's Question: Have people said things to you that have brought you down and stunted an area of growth in your life? In turn have you been privilege to hear words of blessing throughout your life?

Daughter's Question: What would you want to hear your mom say most about who you are in her sight? Your mom needs to be blessed as much as you do; tell her what she does right and do it often.

Agreement: We agree (your signatures) _____ and _____ to bless each other with our words, to go out of our way, and to find times to speak encouragement to each other.

Prayer: Dear Heavenly Father, help us to speak words of encouragement and show love to each other. Amen.

Notes

Blessing:
Attaching High Value

May God give you of Heaven's dew and Earth's
bounty of grain and wine.

Genesis 27:28 (MSG)

In reading *The Blessing* by Gary Smalley and John Trent,
this element made me stop and think about how much
we tend to devalue people, especially without even real-
izing we have done it.

It brought to mind my son. My spoken words are
most often words of value. I see that as my calling from
God—to be an encourager, so it tends to come naturally
for me to bless with my words. But, God opened a window for me to view my own area of weakness when it
came to blessing my son. My son felt most blessed by my
ability to give him my time. When I was a young single
mom, it mattered *a lot* to me what people thought of me.
One of the areas I wanted to impress people with was
my commitment to our community. I showed this commitment by volunteering of my time. One particular area
God showed me was the time I volunteered at the Youth
Emergency Shelter. Admirable? Yes, but not so. This took
time away from my son (when we had very little time
together because as it was I worked a lot), and for what?

To go be with someone else's kids. Don't misunderstand me—I love all kids, it just wasn't the season in my life to feed into other people's children. When raising our children we only get one shot at that season and it is so short to begin with.

I didn't value the time I had with my son and, in turn, didn't show him that I valued him. We have talked about how he needed my time and I have asked for his forgiveness. But it still lingers in my heart today, and I know it affects him in how he handles a lot of elements in his life.

Moms, what are some of the areas you need to seek forgiveness from your kids, or for that matter, your family in general? Take the time to ask them to forgive you for where you haven't valued them. Perhaps you made a promise and didn't keep it. Big or small, keeping your promise shows them they are valued. Or have you spoken a harsh word or been late and not valued someone's time? Daughters, you are not off the hook here—the same applies to you.

Blessing is something we should be doing daily. I know I need to work on valuing my loved ones every day.

Talk Time

 Mother's Question: Where have you felt devalued? What makes you feel you are valued?

 Daughter's Question: Same question as Mom: Where have you felt devalued? What makes you feel you are valued?

Agreement: We (your signatures) _____ and _____ agree to find where we each of us feel valued, and remembering that actions sometimes speak louder than words.

Prayer: Dear Heavenly Father, show us the value in everyone and then help us to show them their value. Amen.

Notes

Blessing: Picturing a Special Future

May nations serve you and peoples bow down to you.

Genesis 27:29 (NIV)

It seemed to be much easier in biblical times to predict your child's future. There weren't as many choices, and most children followed in their parents' footsteps.

Today, there is an abundance of career opportunities and the education system is so vast, with a variety of levels and subjects to choose from. As parents of this generation, we can only open the opportunities for information that will allow them the ability to set meaningful goals for their future achievements.

Our children's future also, however, depends on the words we have spoken into their lives. Words are like the tools used to prepare the soil for planting and harvesting. If we have not tilled the soil for the seeds of education and training to take hold, it will stifle the growth. The element of speaking a special future during a time of blessing is one of the ways in particular you can help them to receive teaching and training. These spoken words will also pave the way for their success.

To share this element of the blessing, you will require insight as to what the future might hold for your children. The best place to start this process is in prayer, asking God to show you what he has in mind for them. Next, watch for their strengths, you can find their strengths while watching them in their everyday routines, keep an eye out for what they excel at. Watch what they enjoy doing, what they do well, and what they seem to do all the time, like singing all day or organizing and keeping their rooms orderly or perhaps encouraging others.

Remember that not only at the time of blessing, but whenever you see them working in their strengths, encourage and compliment them.

My son, for example, had the most wonderful knack for fixing things. He could put stuff together without instructions, and they were always perfect. He struggled with academics, but excelled in this area of craftsmanship. My desire to see him accomplish what God had given him strength in allowed me the ability to let go of pushing so hard in the area of academics. I was able to encourage him in things he did well, and there were many areas besides this one.

Your child's strengths may start to be apparent from as early as two or three. I have seen my granddaughter at a very young age use the awesome gift of leadership (maybe at times needing to be tempered); her friends naturally follow her. She also has a very soft heart, so she is conscious most times, if she is pushing too hard. I speak to the leadership gift in her and often encourage it, but at times bring to her awareness when she may have gone too far. Her mom also has this amazing gift. You will see amazing things once you start focusing on the different strengths in each of your family members.

Just a note: we tend to see weakness much quicker; we believe our job as parents is to teach and mold so we look for places to correct. Remember, we can't always work in our strengths, we need to build our weaknesses, but we need encouragement there—also maybe, even more so. After all she is only human you know.

I write this not only for moms. Daughters you can speak a special future into your mom's life as well. Ask your mom what her dreams for her future are, then speak to those gifts, pray and ask God to provide for your mom. Find times when you see her doing things well and tell her so.

Speaking a special future is just the simple act of encouragement of their strengths along with the discovery of what their desires and dreams are for the future, then speaking to that through words and prayer.

Talk Time

 Mother's Question: Where do you see your strengths? Did anyone ever speak to them when you were a child? What do you see your daughter's strengths are?

 Daughter's Question: Where do you think your strengths are and what do you see as your mom's?

Agreement: We (your signatures) _____ and _____ agree to search out each other's strengths and encourage each other in them and to talk about our desires and dreams for the future on regular bases.

Prayer: Dear Heavenly Father, thank you for giving us each other to encourage and strengthen. Amen.

Notes

Blessing:
An Active Commitment

When I set out from Macedonia, not one church shared with me in the matter of giving and receiving, except you only; for even when I was in Thessalonica, you sent me aid again and again when I was in need.

Philippians 4:15–16 (NIV)

As parents, you have a tremendous role to play in your daughter's future success. This is the part of the blessing where the rubber meets the road. Sometimes, it's easy to speak words of encouragement, but I can tell you, actions speak much louder than words.

There are many things you can do to give your child a fighting chance at success. I am not speaking about worldly success, like climbing the corporate ladder. I am speaking about significance; significance is "knowing the life you lived has eternal rewards." In what areas has God placed your daughter on this Earth to make a difference?

Let's say your daughter shows a gift in the area of music. Easy, right? Provide lessons and make sure they get there and they practice. Ah, but there is more; you need to show her how to use her gifts for the glory of God. Do you want her playing in taverns or such? I don't think so, unless of course God put her there for his greater purpose. She needs to realize her gift is not just for her benefit. When she plays, she plays for an audience of one—God. She will need your help not to look to build herself up, but to be humble, and let her music be a gift to others. Where does your active commitment then start? You will need to find the right instructor, no matter the cost. You will need to take the time and listen to the music she listens to and tries to emulate. You also need to spend time listening to her play. And I am sure you can think of a few more active commitments yourself.

Active commitment takes money and time; are you ready to take the blessing to this level?

Talk Time

 Mother's Question: Was there someone who was actively committed to your success? If so, who and how? If not, what happened because of that?

 Daughter's Question: What do you feel your mom needs to do to help you succeed and what will you do in return?

Agreement: We (your signatures) _____ and _____ agree to be committed to each other's success—not worldly success but Godly significance.

Prayer: Dear Heavenly Father, thank you for giving us the ability to bless through active commitment. Help us to follow through. Help us make our words a matter of action. Amen.

Tips for Blessing
Our Children

Esau pleaded, "But do you have only one blessing? Oh my father, bless me, too!" Then Esau broke down and wept.

Genesis 27:38 (NLT)

"You are ready!" We have looked at all the elements for a successful time of blessing for your children. Don't let this information overwhelm you. If you take time to seek God he will give you all you need, I promise. You are only the vessel used to pour out blessing.

So let's start planning this special occasion. The environment in which you perform your blessing is important. Think of any important celebration you have attended or planned, and you will remember the time that was taken to decorate and prepare the menu. I think you might have your daughter's attention now (most girls I know love planning celebrations)—ask her what she would like. You don't have to spend a lot of money to make it festive. Use what you have at home and be creative.

Mom, if you have more than one child, you need to make sure they are all blessed. Each child is unique, so each blessing will need to have something special for each of them. Daughters, please remember your parents need your blessing take time to create a special blessing; for them, too.

So just to recap how to provide a "Time of Blessing":

- Incorporate touch in your blessing. Hold their hand, hug them, whatever is comfortable for both of you.

- Spoken word. Prepare what you are going to say ahead of time. Think it through, pray, and ask God to give you the words they need to hear. Remember, they need to hear your praise often. This is not a "one time and you're done" deal, like the man who said he loved his wife on their wedding day and never said it again. When asked why, he said, "I told her on our wedding day that I loved her, and if anything changes, I'll let her know." This story should not be yours.

- Attach high value. Everyone needs to know they are valued, not for what they do, but for who God made them to be. Each person has a way that they receive value—you will just need to discover how (tips for this will be covered in our section on love languages; watch for our next ninety-day conversation starter).

- Speak into their future. Encourage their gifts and strengths. You can't only speak this once and expect to see them soar. You need to believe in them always and tell them that you do.

- An active commitment. Actions always speak louder than words. The promises you make them at the time of their blessing needs to be acted upon. Make the effort to help them in any way possible so they will grow into the person God has created them to be.

Here are some tips to help you prepare what you want to say in your blessing:

- First, ask God to help you speak a blessing into your child's life.

- When we bless our children, we bless them for who they are, not what they do. Make sure to separate their identity from their behaviour.

- Let them know they are wanted in your home and why.

- Let them know something about their birth and the excitement around that.

- Let them know that they do not belong to you, but God has blessed you with the awesome opportunity to look after them and raise them. Their Heavenly Father is their ultimate Father and you entrust them into his care.

- Take this time to ask for forgiveness; search your heart, and ask God what needs to be addressed, or, where your daughter may have felt wronged.

- It is always powerful to speak Scripture over your child when blessing them. Find scriptures of God's promises. One of my favorites is Jeremiah 29:11.

Girls, take note, some day, you will have children of your own and you too will need to bless them. Also, remember your parents need you to bless them as well.

It is not so important to do it formally, but your words matter, so speak words that build your parents up not tear them down.

It excites me to envision all the blessing that will transpire from reading this information. Thank you for applying this amazing ceremony into your family's life.

Talk Time

 Mother's Question: Looking back over the last few days, what part of the blessing stands out the most for you?

 Daughter's Question: Same question as Mom. What part of the blessing stands out the most for you?

Agreement: We (your signatures) _____ and _____ agree to look for the blessing in each other and speak it frequently—to incorporate this biblical truth of blessings into our family traditions.

Prayer: Dear Heavenly Father, thank you for teaching us about blessing. Keep our words and actions expressing our love for each other. Amen

Moms Need to be Blessed Too

'Honor your father and mother'–which is the first commandment with promise–'so that it may go well with you and that you may enjoy long life on the earth." Fathers, do not exasperate your children; instead, bring them up in the training and instruction of the Lord.'

Ephesians 6:2–4 (NIV)

Well, daughters, you and I need to talk, and yes, Mom, you can listen in. I have to tell you that I don't see many girls blessing their moms very often. I know at this time of your life you have become inner-focused. Yes, you think it is all about you, but guess what? God wired you that way. You are in discovery mode, and this is good. I want to caution you, though; it can take over your whole being. At this stage in your life, you are living for today; the future hasn't registered yet. If you are fortunate enough to have a mom who understands this and has unconditional love for you (which I believe all of you do if you are reading this book with your mom), then your relationship will remain strong.

If I could encourage you to step back daily and ask yourself this, "Who have I blessed today?" "When have

I taken the focus off my wants and needs and looked at someone else's need to be blessed?" I'll bet you that you will answer this most times with a blessing that you have given to a friend, not your mom or family members.

See, you know that your mom will always love you, and you also believe that she will always be around. Because of this, you may take your mom for granted. Please take the time to look at what your mom might need to have done for her or what words she might need to hear. I know your mom would give her life for you. Take the time to give her a piece of yours. Find out what blesses her most and go out of your way to do it. I can guarantee your mom very seldom hears from you what a great mom she is; leave her a note today.

Talk Time

Mother's Question: Do you feel you could be blessed more often? Don't shy away or be all humble, speak up; your daughter needs to know.

Daughter's Question: Ask your mom what makes her feel good, give her some examples: a hug, a note, a thank you, you know what to ask.

Agreement: I (daughter only) _____ agree to bless my mom regularly.

Prayer: Dear Heavenly Father, thank you for my mom. She is a great gift; help me to bless her. Amen.

Knowing the Opposite of Blessing

But God told Balaam, "Do not go with them. You are not to curse these people, for they have been blessed!"

Numbers 22:12 (NLT)

It is important to understand what the opposite of blessing is: it is a curse, to speak harsh words that seep into a person's being and in turn alters their life.

I know beyond a shadow of a doubt that harsh words spoken in anger are not always meant. I, too, sometimes have a sharp tongue. I have spent many a day working through this and have come a long way. But, what about those curses I spoke unknowingly? Like you need to do, I have had to ask for forgiveness.

There are also those times when we knowingly speak harsh words and the same applies—we must ask for forgiveness. In both cases, you need to assure people that what you have said is not true. That we are all perfectly and wonderfully made (as the Bible tells us), that our actions are not our identity, and that the person we are is good. Doing this releases the curse you had spoken over their lives.

I can still remember things said to me from people who didn't even really know me or even those who knew me well. Kids in school, my friends, and even my family who made fun of me or criticized me spoke curses over my life.

In a lot of cases I don't even remember the names of those who spoke in a negative way about my weight, my looks, my intelligence, or my abilities. Their words stuck, but, their names didn't. It is hard at times to deal with the fact that they will probably not never ask for my forgiveness or tell me that what they said was not true. This makes it my job to forgive them on my own and to expose their words for what they are: "a curse on who I am," "a lie", and then to discard them from my life. How, you ask? Through what I think about who I am. I am a cherished daughter of the King of Kings.

There are also the curses that come from unresolved conflict. The most dangerous are those which happen in our families. They usually appear through serious family conflicts. By serious family conflicts, I mean conflicts that result in unpleasant words being said against a family member after which both or one of them hold bitterness against the other. Serious family conflicts that are not reconciled will result in distressing experiences in the spiritual, social, physical, and material realms. Curses may also come from friends in the same way.

To release a curse from your life is as simple as becoming aware that a curse exists, then pray and ask God to remove it. Now you need only to believe in God's truth of who you are, a cherished daughter of the King of Kings. In John 8:32, it says, "Then you will know the truth, and the truth will set you free." You are now free! Remember your freedom came at a price through grace of our Lord. You need to reciprocate that grace to all who have cursed you.

Talk Time

 Mother's Question: Was there someone who spoke a curse over your life? If so, how did it affect you? Have you released the curse and the person who spoke it?

 Daughter's Question: Is there someone you know who has said something to you that hurts? If there is, pray now and ask for God's truth and for the ability to forgive them.

Agreement: We (your signatures) _____ and _____ agree to watch our tongues and speak only blessings. When we speak a curse, we will ask for forgiveness. If we are harbouring a curse, we will see it for what it is and pray for God's release.

Prayer: Dear Heavenly Father, thank you for helping us to speak words of encouragement and love to everyone. Thank you for showing us the danger of cursing people and enlightening us as to any curses we may have held on to. Show us how to release them and move on. Amen.

Notes

A Little Insight into
the Cause of Anger

For our struggle is not against flesh and blood,
but against the rulers, against the authorities,
against the powers of this dark world and against
the spiritual forces of evil in the heavenly realms.

Ephesians 6:12–13 (NIV)

Many things can spark anger in us. Some of our anger is just and when directed properly can be healthy. When we see injustices in the world, our anger is well-founded and should call us to action, although we must always remember God is the judge; the punishment is his, not ours. Our desire should be to see reconciliation for mankind so not one should perish.

Let's talk a little bit about defensiveness and relational anger; it can be in our families or between friends. Ever wonder why, when you say something to someone, they take what you said and do a 180 degree turn-around on it? You know yourself that is not what you meant. So how does that happen? My example is something I used to do constantly and still sometimes resort to and that is being defensive. I would take what someone had said, and no matter how innocent the comment, turn it into a need to make what was being addressed not my fault. This is where some of our relational anger starts.

Satan will take things that are said to us and use our past experiences or subtle lies where we may be insecure to create an unfounded anger in us. This will cause hurt and offense to take place in our relationships. Hurt and offense will then turn into a bitterroot that will harden our hearts and destroying our most important relationships. Satan's desire is to see disunity. He knows that within unity of relationships God's plan can succeed.

We have to fight our battles as the Bible instructs us, "We are not to fight flesh against flesh, but the spiritual forces controlling this world." So what does that mean? Well, without getting into some heavy theological stuff, I know you are aware that God is love and he wants all good things for you. He is our protector. With that, what is he protecting us from? He is protecting us from ourselves and other humans, but even more so from that is the unseen spiritual forces. As Christians, we all know we have an enemy—the father of lies. He would love nothing more than to have our relationships in turmoil so that what God has called us to do in that relationship will never be accomplished.

The next time your anger is getting the best of you, remember to fight the real enemy—"Satan." Just remember though, you cannot fight Satan alone; only through the name of Jesus will you be victorious.

Talk Time

Mother's Question: Can you remember a time when you said something or something was said to you that was taken out of context? Where do you think that lie came from?

Daughter's Question: Same as Mom: Can you remember a time when you said something or something was said to you that it was taken out of context? Where do you think that lie came from?

Agreement: We (your signatures) _____ and _____ agree to fight our conflicts in the spirit realm, not in the flesh. To desire unity and not judge to allow God to take his rightful place—he will judge.

Prayer: Dear Heavenly Father, thank you for the authority you gave us over Satan; help us to use our authority that you have given to remove any unhealthy anger. Amen.

Notes

_____

_____

_____

_____

_____

_____

_____

_____

_____

_____

_____

_____

_____

_____

_____

_____

Is Anger Okay with God?

And "don't sin by letting anger control you." Don't let the sun go down while you are still angry, for anger gives a foothold to the devil.

Ephesians 4:26–27 (NLT)

Did you know that anger can be a good thing, done the right way for the right reasons? It's found in the divine nature of God. It's what we do with our anger that makes it wrong or right.

The essence of anger is to have the feeling of disgust when injustice is done. A good example of this is the program MADD (Mothers Against Drunk Drivers). This program was developed by a mom whose child was killed by a drunk driver.

Her anger has helped to make the roads a safer place, not only for children, but for everyone. So do you think she was mad at the person driving that vehicle under the influence of alcohol? For sure! Instead of taking that anger and doing something awful to that person or just becoming an angry person and hurting those she loves, she used her anger to create a positive difference for thousands of people. In a way, she made the world a better place. That's a good use of anger, wouldn't you say?

You might be saying, "Ya, but, I haven't had to feel that kind of anger, and the things I get angry at aren't something that I could turn into a 'change the world' opportunity." I'd like to give you some food for thought.

Let's take this simple example of anger: Mom, you are angry at your daughter because she disobeyed you and went to a party. You take that anger and you turn it towards your daughter personally. Weeks go by, and you still haven't let it go. Let me ask you, what do you think the environment in your home has been like? This one event is wedging a space into your relationship. Your daughter is now not feeling loved or forgiven. Your anger is now pushing your daughter to the point that she doesn't like being home. Can you see where this is leading to? Your anger is a seed that is growing out of control, it is being watered by unforgiveness and bitterness. All the relationships in your life are being affected in some way by this one event. The old saying "we hurt the people we love most"—even when it isn't their fault. May I also remind you it was an event, not a person, who created this anger. We are not what we do, but who God made us. So yes, unhealthy anger could change the world because the most important world you have is your circle of influence.

Talk Time

 Mother's Question: Talk about a time your anger has caused an undesirable outcome. How would you have liked to change that?

 Daughter's Question: What are things that make you angry? How do you react? What would you like to change?

Agreement: We (your signatures) _____ and _____ agree to keep our anger intact.

Prayer: Dear Heavenly Father, thank you for giving us anger. Show us how to use our anger for your glory. Amen.

Notes

_____

_____

_____

_____

_____

_____

_____

_____

_____

_____

_____

_____

_____

_____

_____

_____

Mission Statements

"For I know the plans I have for you,' declares the Lord, 'plans to prosper you and not to harm you, plans to give you hope and a future".

Jeremiah 29:11 (NIV)

Today, we are going to start to look at mission statements. As you know, I work as a business and life coach, and one of the first things I take a client through is designing their business mission statement. A mission statement will guide a company in good times and bad. A meaningful mission statement can act as a moral and corporate compass. It can help you make decisions aligned with your values and goals.

I know you're thinking, "So what does that have to do with me?" My thought has always been that if a mission statement is so important for a company, why not for people? As I researched, prayed, and pondered on this thought, I have come to realize that if we stand for nothing, we will fall for anything; hence the need for a life mission statement.

Earlier, we looked at finding your personal calling; this will form part of your mission statement but certainly not all of it.

Let's start by examining some of the facts about mission statements.

To start with, a good mission statement should be short and to the point. One sentence is usually enough. You want to be able to recall it and state it concisely whenever the need arises. Remember, anyone should be able to understand it—even a child. Don't use such eloquent and complex words that it makes you seem like you are prideful or better than others.

The Mission Statements below are from famous people in history. The statements are short and to the point, but within them these people did amazing things:

- Abraham Lincoln's mission was to preserve the Union.

- Mother Teresa's mission was to show mercy and compassion to the dying.

- Joan of Arc's mission was to free France.

- Nehemiah's mission was to rebuild the walls of Jerusalem.

Your mission statements are inclusive of but not in total;

"Your current employment"

"The things on your to-do list"

"Your ministry"

"Your family"

"Your strengths"

"Your talents"

Your mission statement may be as simple and yet important as "I am raising my family to be Godly leaders." Nothing is ever too small; within small mission statements, there are amazing results. Think of all Mother Teresa did in her life and yet her mission statement only says to show mercy and compassion to the dying.

Note: Daughters, it is never too early to know your mission statement. Joan of Arc heard hers at twelve years old!

God has created all of us for a purpose; we are here on earth for a reason. Believe me when I say, he can provide you with all that you need to achieve what he has called you to do.

Envision Henry Ford and his creation of the first automobile. When he set to the plan, he didn't think "the automobile would keep people warm at night." No, he thought this automobile will transport people from one place to another. As Henry Ford had a plan for the car, God designed you with a plan for your life.

My Mission statement: *I help people to be leaders not followers through the educated choices they make.*

While you're pondering your mission statement, don't forget, the most important part of finding the answer is to ask your designer God.

Talk Time

 Mother's Question: Do you have a mission statement? Do you know what God has planned for you to do while you are here on Earth?

 Daughter's Question: What are things you most enjoy doing? What comes easy for you? These may be clues that will help you design your mission statement.

Agreement: We (your signatures) _____ and
_____ agree to pray and search for God's plan
for our lives, "our mission statement." Then to live it out
according to his glory.

Prayer: Dear Heavenly Father, help us not to spend our
days selfishly looking to fill our wants, but help us to see
what you have called us here on earth to do. Amen.

Family Mission Statement

But as for me and my family, we will serve the Lord.

Joshua 24:15 (NLT)

It might be beneficial to skip this day until such a time as, Mom, you have had time to review this information with your husband. Once you have had that opportunity, have your whole family read through and discuss this information together.

Do you think it was an accident that you were put together as a family? Personally, I don't think so. Just as you were put here on Earth to complete something that the Father has sent you to do, so it is that your family fits into that puzzle. Together, your family unit has a mission only it can fulfill and each member has a vital part to play.

In his book *7 Habits of Effective Families*, Stephen Covey gives some great wisdom for families, including building a family mission statement. Let me share some of his insights coupled with a few of my own.

A family mission statement is a combined, unified expression from all family members as to what your family is all about—what it really wants to do or be and the principle/values you choose to govern your family life.

Before you start designing your family mission statement, you should perhaps discuss your family values. They are desirable qualities, standards, or principles. Values are the family's driving force that influence your actions and reactions. To discover your family's values, have a discussion on what as a family you would not want to see a member experience or act on. Then as a family what you most value in life. Write this information down as it will help you to form your family mission statement.

Here are some further questions to drive your discussion in designing your family mission statement.

Pose these questions to each member of your family. Have them write their answers and then share those answers with each other. The most important rules for sharing these questions are that there is no criticizing each other's answers. You must be open to all input and find ways to include everyone's valuable input. Think of it in terms of a brainstorming session where all input is valued and broken down. Don't forget to ask the why question: "Why do you feel this is important?"

- What is the essential mission or purpose of our family (why do you think you as a family exist)?

- Is there a cause or a group that your family is passionate about? What type of needs do you think they would have? What are some ways you as a family could help in these areas?

- What is our family about?

- What are our highest priorities and goals?

You are now ready to start the process of creating the first draft of your Family Mission Statement. Take all your answers and word—smith it into a family mission statement. Oh, wait first, I am going to ask you as a family and individually to pray and ask for God's for input. Don't rush this process. Note that whatever you come up with is not set in stone; over time, it may evolve and change. God is always doing a new thing.

Just as a sample, here is our family mission statement (which is ever evolving) "to build unity and trust, helping people have a place where they feel they belong in a family that loves the Lord our God first."

Take your completed family mission statement and post it somewhere that everyone can see it. Read it together regularly; weave into the very fiber of your family.

Talk Time

Mother's Question: Before you married, did you ever discuss with your future husband about what your family mission would be?

Daughter's Question: What is the one thing you see most in your family? For example: generosity, a heart for the underprivileged, or perhaps a political calling.

Agreement: As a family, initial here_____ We agree to pray and search for God's plan for our family as a unit and then strive to achieve it.

Prayer: Dear Heavenly Father, help us to hear you regarding what our family is to do together as a mission for you here on earth and then to accomplish it. Amen.

Notes

Marriage Mission Statement

> Do two people walk hand in hand if they aren't
> going to the same place?
>
> Amos 3:3 (MSG)

It is so common for girls to dream of their wedding day. Right from the time they start school and even perhaps before then, they are dressing up and creating that special day.

My granddaughter (at seven years old) and her girlfriends love to use my dress-up clothes and create the perfect wedding, flowers and all. They have even convinced the little guy across the street to be the groom. He is, of course, much younger than all of them because boys their age will have nothing to do with this game, and at Grandma's house, there is no kissing the bride.

So let me ask, if they are already dreaming of their wedding day, wouldn't it be prudent to teach them about the days after the wedding—their marriage? They are never too young for you to take the time to teach them about and model for them God's most sacred gift: the union between husband and wife.

It is never too early to share with daughters the importance of having a marriage mission statement. Our daughters walk down the aisle with more than a bouquet of flowers; they walk down that aisle with their dreams and expectations. As you know, shortly after your wedding day, reality hits life, and there is no turning back. We are now married until death do us part.

If we can train our daughters up for marriage success before their wedding day, we will help them to build a strong foundation for marriage and save them much heartache. Sharing important and truthful marriage tips as they walk the journey from young ladies to women ready for marriage will prepare them to be Godly wives.

The best way to help them succeed at marriage is for you have a great marriage yourself. Invest in your marriage; learn all you can about marriage. There are great resources out there.

For today, we will start with a marriage mission statement; it is a tool that gives your marriage a foundation to build on. If you haven't one from the beginning, there is no time like the present to get started.

Your statement should consist of both your dreams and aspirations coming together to move in the same direction for God's glory. If you are always fighting to go your separate ways, there won't be a union; therefore it is not a marriage. It doesn't mean you need to be the same—God doesn't want you to be the same because if you were one of you wouldn't be needed—but he does want you to go in the same direction. A marriage mission statement will help you to be on the same page, helping each other to finish the race and run it well.

So here are some questions to think about when creating your marriage mission statement:

- What was in God's heart when he brought us together?

- What individual strengths do you have that complement each other?

- What are the areas you struggle in which you could turn from your calling?

- How can you help each other be the best you can be?

- What expectations do you have of each other? Are they fair? What happens if you fall short of meeting them?

- What commitments can you make to each other that will make sure divorce is never an option?

Moms, this probably spoke more to you, but this day is the start of that journey to prepare your precious daughter for her most significant relationship after you and God—her future marriage. Daughters, it is never too early to start thinking about what you would want in your marriage mission statement—answer the above questions, even hypothetically (in other words, dream about your marriage).

Talk Time

 Mother's Question: Do you have a marriage mission statement? If not, are you ready to work with your husband to design one?

 Daughter's Question: Have you thought about what you and your husband will accomplish together?

Agreement: We (your signatures) _____ and _____ agree that God has created marriage for a greater purpose and that we want to have our marriages fulfill what God has designed them for.

Prayer: Dear Heavenly Father, help us to hear you clearly as to what our marriage is to accomplish. Then give us the courage, wisdom, and strength to live that out. Amen.

Your Value Statement

A good person produces good things from the treasury of a good heart, and an evil person produces evil things from the treasury of an evil heart.

Luke 6:45 NLT

Values are desirable qualities, standards, or principles. Values are a person's driving force, and they influence their actions and reactions.

Saying, "He's a courageous man," or "She's a generous woman," reflects a person's deepest priorities in life. A brave man speaks out, even when it's dangerous to do so. A generous woman selflessly gives money or her time to help others.

Everyone has personal values, even if they don't realize it. You inherit some of your values. You learn some values from your parents, your church, your teachers, and other influential people in your life. You also take on values from reading books and watching TV and then of course from the school-of-hard-knocks life experiences.

Your values will tend to be fairly concrete, although they may undergo some changes as you gain more wisdom throughout your life. Why is it important to know what your values are? It is simple—so you can make better choices.

People who don't know what their values are tend to wander around, bouncing from one thing to another, trying to find themselves. They're like puppets, pulled by others who have set their values, either bad or good.

Creating Your Value Statement

Below, you will find a list of words that will help you to create your value system. If you are anything like me, it is so hard to come up with words just off the top of my head. This list is not complete; it is just to get your mind working and to give you some examples. Take the time to evaluate the words below; you want to make sure the ones you choose are ones that you know what they mean. Once you have done that, choose the words which best stand for what you believe your values are. Remember, values are desirable qualities, standards, or principles. Values are a person's driving force, and they influence their actions and reactions. The best scenario is to bring your list down to three. Once you have the words that most state your values, create a statement using all three.

For example, my personal value statement reads, "My life will be an example of seeking wisdom and creating unity among all." Your newly-designed statement is now a guard for the way you live your life. Until it becomes embedded in your heart and mind, place your statement where you can read it often. Once you have it memorized, it will help you have parameters and guidelines for your actions. You're less likely to take the easy way out or chase after short-term gains at the expense of your long-term goals.

Like the saying goes, those who stand for nothing fall for anything, so use your value statement to help set your boundaries and to guide your future.

Accomplishment, Success	Family feeling	Prosperity, Wealth
Accountability	Flair	Punctuality
Accuracy	Freedom	Quality of work
Adventure	Friendship	Regularity
All for one & one for all	Fun	Reliability
Beauty	Global view	Resourcefulness
Calm, quietude, peace	Good will	Respect for others
Challenge Change	Goodness	Responsiveness
Cleanliness, orderliness	Gratitude	Results-oriented
Collaboration	Hard work	Rule of Law
Commitment	Harmony	Safety
Communication	Honesty	Satisfying others
Community	Honor	Security
Competence	Improvement	Self-givingness
Competition	Independence	Self-reliance
Concern for others	Individuality	Self-thinking
Connection	Inner peace, calm, quietude	Service (to others, society)
Content over form	Innovation	Simplicity
Continuous improvement	Integrity	Skill
Cooperation	Intensity	Solving Problems
Coordination	Justice	Speed
Creativity	Knowledge	Spirit in life (using)
Customer satisfaction	Leadership	Stability
Decisiveness	Love, Romance	Standardization
Delight of being, joy	Loyalty	Status
Democracy	Maximum utilization (of time, resources)	Strength
Discipline	Meaning	Succeed; A will to- Success, Achievement
Discovery	Merit	Systemization
Diversity	Money	Teamwork
Ease of Use	Openness	Timeliness
Efficiency	Patriotism	Tolerance
Equality	Peace, Non-violence	Tradition
Excellence	Perfection	Tranquility
Fairness	Personal Growth	Trust
Faith	Pleasure	Truth
Faithfulness	Power	Unity
Family	Practicality	Variety
	Preservation	Wisdom
	Privacy	
	Progress	

Talk Time

 Mother's Question: What values do you wish you had set when you were younger, before you made some of your decisions?

 Daughter's Question: Who is a friend you admire? What would you say her most visible value is?

Agreement: We (your signatures) _____ and _____ agree to discuss what our values are and to help each other implement them into our day-to-day lives.

Prayer: Dear Heavenly Father, help us to find in your word the values we are to have as followers of you. Amen.

The Fight Against Your Set Mission and Values

There is a wide-open door for a great work here, although many oppose me.

1 Corinthians 16:9 (NLT)

Once you have accomplished the task of putting your mission and value statements on paper, the act of living it daily will be an ongoing struggle. Remember though, if there is no struggle with the disciplines of living for what you believe, the rewards will be meaningless.

Satan is opposed to any effort you will make to live a life of purpose and strong values, ones according to God's design. He will use whatever he can; people, situations, and your own thought life to stop you from achieving what God has planned for you.

Unfortunately, people will try to dissuade you from walking out what you have set your life to be according to your statements. When people have no set values or purpose, they are uncomfortable with someone who does. Instead of them feeling judged or guilty by the way you live your life, they will work at changing what you believe. You will have to be aware of people's influence on your standards, and if you can't stand for what you believe in when around those certain people, you will have to distance yourself from them.

Satan will also use things like the burden of shame if he can catch you when you have made a mistake or gotten off track; he will forever throw that at you. When you release that shame and follow closer to Jesus and listen to what the Bible teaches, you will become aware of how Satan tries to blind you from the truth. If he can keep you from all God has for you, he wins, and not only that, but you could lead others down that same path of destruction.

There will be times when Satan will make situations (like parties and such) look "oh-so-appealing", but be on your guard. If these places will compromise your values or they don't enhance or feed your life mission, stay away! It will be hard, the desire will be strong, but think on this: "the consequence of that situation or place may last a lifetime."

Know that you have an enemy. The Bible says Satan has come to kill, steal, and destroy, and you have the only weapon you need to have him flee from your life: the name of Jesus.

I have complete confidence in you that you are able to achieve all that is planned for you. Your life's call has been placed in you by your Creator, and no one can ever take that away. Remember, though, God gave you free will, and he will never step in and take it away. This means that only your decisions can hinder your purpose here on earth.

Talk Time

Mother's Question: Is there a time in your life when Satan has steered you the wrong way? What were the consequences of that?

Daughter's Question: Where is your toughest battle happening right now?

Agreement: We (your signatures) _____ and _____ agree to help each other follow through with keeping our mission and value statements alive and working in our lives.

Prayer: Dear Heavenly Father, help keep our eyes focused on you and help us to fight the enemy. Amen.

Notes

_____

_____

_____

_____

_____

_____

_____

_____

_____

_____

_____

_____

_____

_____

_____

The Fight for Self-Discipline

> I don't know about you, but I'm running hard for the finish line. I'm giving it everything I've got. No sloppy living for me! I'm staying alert and in top condition. I'm not going to get caught napping, telling everyone else all about it and then missing out myself.
>
> 1 Corinthians 9:26–27 (MSG)

Self-discipline is the ability to get yourself to take action, regardless of your emotional state. Imagine what you could accomplish if you could simply get yourself to follow through on your best intentions, no matter what. Vince Lombardi once said, "The difference between a successful person and others is not a lack of strength, not a lack of knowledge, but rather a lack of will."

I can promise you that self-discipline is hard to achieve. There are areas of my life where I still struggle, and I have been working on this for fifty or more years. I can also promise you, it is one of the most rewarding things in life. When you have accomplished what you have set out to do and stuck to it no matter what, the feeling of achievement is a great high.

There are many times in this life where you will have to have self-discipline (especially when it comes to purity), and the earlier you start training yourself, the better. Did you know that building self-discipline is like training a muscle: the more you work it, the stronger it gets.

Just to get you thinking about what level of self-discipline you may have, I have provided a test below in "Talk Time."

Talk Time

For today's discussion, here is a list of daily routines that require some level of self-discipline. On a scale of 1–10 (1 being low, 10 being high), rate your overall level of self-discipline for the following tasks.

Daughters, there may be a few questions you are unable to answer—not to worry, answer what you can.

- Do you shower or bath daily?
- Are you able to get up when your alarm goes off the first time?
- Do you sleep the weekends away?
- Do you struggle with dieting?
- Are there addictions (caffeine, nicotine, sugar, etc.) you'd like to break but haven't?
- Are you current on all your e-mails?
- Is your office neat and well-organized?
- Is your home neat and well-organized?
- Is your room neat and well-organized?
- How much time do you waste in a typical day (perhaps watching TV or playing computer games, texting or on social media sites).

- If you make a promise to someone, will you keep it?

- If you promise yourself something, will you keep it?

- Would you be able to fast for one day?

- Do you exercise regularly?

- Do you fail to complete your homework on a regular basis?

- Do you complete the priority items on your to-do list?

- Do you have clear, written goals for all areas of your life?

- Do you have a plan on how to achieve them?

- Could you give up TV for a month?

- Are you happy with the way you look right now (what does your appearance say about your level of discipline—clothes, grooming, etc.)?

- Do you eat healthy most times?

- Have you adopted a positive new habit or stopped a bad habit?

- Do you spend most of your money on items you won't have in the next year?

- Are you in debt—do you live paycheck to paycheck?

- Do you know what you'll be doing tomorrow/next weekend?

Now, congratulate each other on the areas where you're doing well. Then discuss the areas you struggle in—help each other to create a plan to strengthen your discipline muscle. Continue to encourage each other as it is a fight to stay disciplined.

Agreement: We (your signatures) _____ and _____ agree to help each other with our self-discipline. We will gently remind each other of times when we may be slipping and encourage each other to get back on track.

Prayer: Dear Heavenly Father, help us to stick to things we have committed to do. We want to be women of our word and to be able to practice self-discipline to achieve the life you have designed for us. Amen.

Dream Big

> Now to him who is able to do immeasurably more than all we ask or imagine, according to his power that is at work within us, to him be glory in the church and in Christ Jesus throughout all generations, forever and ever! Amen.
>
> Ephesians 3:20–21 (NIV)

I attended a session with Peter Daniels (you can find out more about him by Googling his name) where he taught about the power to dream. He asked the following question:

Close your eyes and dream of whatever you want to have, anything in this world. List the first three things that come to your mind. Then, out of the three, what would be the one thing you would want most?

So what did you come up with? I bet you didn't dream big enough. I'll give you an example of what one person said at the Peter Daniels conference —"I would like to travel around the world and see every sight there is to see." When they answered the question, this is what Peter said, "I told you, you could have anything in the world. That means money and time are of no concern. So not only could you travel, you could take everyone with you." *Dream bigger*!

Satan has robbed us of our ability to see how big our God is. God has made everything, and his plans for his children are more than we can imagine. We have set our own limits by listening to what people have said to us, about us and about our failures. We take those things that have been said and let them limit what we believe we can accomplish.

Don't limit your dreams. God has a plan for your life. As big as you can dream, he will dream bigger. Let yourselves believe, and he will provide all you need. Friendly reminder: wants and needs are different. God knows what you need, and it is not always what you want.

	1	2	3	4	5	6	7	8	9	10
Personal Requirements what you already have, think in the past)										
Imagination (is to envision it)	❏	❏	❏	❏	❏	❏	❏	❏	❏	❏
Pressure (what types of pressure come with your dream)	❏	❏	❏	❏	❏	❏	❏	❏	❏	❏
Perception (how well have you dealt with your past decisions)	❏	❏	❏	❏	❏	❏	❏	❏	❏	❏
Daring (your ability to take risks	❏	❏	❏	❏	❏	❏	❏	❏	❏	❏
Basic Requirements (think in the present, what you have now)										
Desire	❏	❏	❏	❏	❏	❏	❏	❏	❏	❏
Ability	❏	❏	❏	❏	❏	❏	❏	❏	❏	❏
Work Ethic	❏	❏	❏	❏	❏	❏	❏	❏	❏	❏
Knowledge	❏	❏	❏	❏	❏	❏	❏	❏	❏	❏
Limiting Factors look into the future and think of ways to overcome these obstacles to meet your dream)										
Cash	❏	❏	❏	❏	❏	❏	❏	❏	❏	❏
Planning	❏	❏	❏	❏	❏	❏	❏	❏	❏	❏
World View	❏	❏	❏	❏	❏	❏	❏	❏	❏	❏
Potential	❏	❏	❏	❏	❏	❏	❏	❏	❏	❏

Talk Time

 Mother's Question: What were your dreams growing up? Where there dreams you never lived? Is it maybe time?

 Daughter's Question: What are some of the things you dream about doing, seeing or having?

Agreement: We (your signatures) _____ and _____ agree to help each other dream big and achieve it. We will be each other's dream cheerleader.

Prayer: Dear Heavenly Father, help us to claim our dreams, and God-size them, then please help us achieve them. Amen.

Notes

What Do Dreams Have to Do with Purity?

No eye has seen, no ear has heard, and no mind has imagined what God has prepared for those who love him.

1 Corinthians 2:9 (NLT)

There is a caution to dreaming: it is that your life can be consumed by it. Unfortunately, most of our culture is steeped in a dream life. Consider lottery tickets people dream about winning and how great their life would be with all that money. Money doesn't change your life, Jesus does.

For women especially, we need to be careful what we talk about, read, and watch on TV. We can stress about or romance everything. Dreaming does not mean to live outside reality or to wish things away. The Bible is clear: we are to be content in where we are today, not to worry for our future.

I recently had to check myself. The books I happened to be reading had a romantic twist to them. The words of these books were weaving dreams of expectations for how my husband should be treating me. I was wondering why he couldn't be as romantic as the men in the stories. It was amazing when the Lord showed me this; he took me to thoughts and actions I had taken because of what I was reading. My husband is wonderfully romantic, just not every day.

I quickly switched my reading. I am now reading Christian stories of times long gone by; the stories of husbands and wives who were pioneers. How their relationships had to stand through tough times and their love was strengthened through those time. I have that kind of love with my husband. I can now see that in reading those other books, Satan used them to make me dissatisfied in my marriage and I took the bait.

Watch for Satan's tactics, question if your dreams are from him or from God. Dreams created by unhealthy worldly influences such as the books I was reading are damaging to the purity of your mind, body, and spirits. Avoid them at all costs.

At times, we will settle or believe we don't deserve to have the dreams God has implanted in our hearts. We get in a rush. We feel like failures. We don't see things for what they really are. Just because of this, we will throw our dreams out the window. God has a plan, a dream for you; it's so important for you to trust God and let him in. If you do, the dreams he has for your life will come true.

Take the time to dream of what living a life of purity (mind, body, spirit) would look like. How would living a life of purity affect who you are and your future?

For those who have struggled with living a life of purity and think that you can only dream of what might have been, I want to remind you that Satan is limiting your ability to dream and achieve purity. We profess with our mouths that Jesus died for our sins and washed us clean as snow (perfectly white). Let your dreams begin right here, and then let God direct your steps. Purity starts right where you are today!

Talk Time

Mother's Question: Was there anyone in your life that taught you about purity and helped you dream about living a life based on purity?

Daughter's Question: Discuss with your mom what a life of purity might look like.

Agreement: We (your signatures) _____ and _____ agree to dream together of what a pure life might look like and then to ask God to help us achieve a future of purity.

Prayer: Dear Heavenly Father, show us the plans you have for our awesome future, a future of purity. Amen.

Notes

What the Right Attitude Can Do

Work willingly at whatever you do, as though you were working for the Lord rather than for people. Remember that the Lord will give you an inheritance as your reward, and that the Master you are serving is Christ.

Colossians 3:23–24 (NLT)

My husband made a profound statement; at least it was for me. He said, "If I have to do something, I might as well enjoy doing it."

I can think of many times I have taken on a task and grumbled all the way through doing it. So where did that get me? Irritated, upset, and probably taking it out on everyone around me. The task still got done, but it took so much energy to stay in my funk that the task took longer to do and usually didn't produce the best of results.

Girls, you first: can you think of a time your parents asked you to do something and you grumbled through the whole task and then all day? Maybe it was cleaning your room. Moms, I know beyond a doubt we are no better. Ever thought "another night where I have to cook dinner, and no one appreciates how much effort goes into preparing meals." Have you perhaps even said something like that lately?

We don't always have control over what has to be done, but we do have control over how we choose to feel about it. I have seen evidence of this in effect. Before we had a dishwasher, I happened to be the one always responsible to do dishes. Back then, I let those in my home do very little. I cursed, (yes cursed!) the fact that I had to stand over a sink every night by myself and wash everyone's dirty dishes. My blood pressure must have been so high I could have skyrocketed. That night, it was like Jesus came right into that room and said to me, "You are not doing those dishes for anyone but me, this is an act of service for those you love and I am well pleased." From then on, any time I did the dishes, I felt the joy of Jesus as he watched me sacrifice even that little bit.

Whatever you feed your mind will grow; if you give it anger, contention, and disharmony, that's what it will create. If you want joy, peace and love, think on those things while attending to all your tasks. Be thankful in all you do, remembering perhaps that you have a room to clean or food to eat that created those dirty dishes. I too am not perfect yet, I have to work at this daily and so will you.

Talk Time

 Mother's Question: Are there chores that you take on that you don't do joyfully? How can you change this?

 Daughter's Question: What do you hate most to do, and how do you think you can turn that around?

Agreement: We (your signatures) _____ and _____ agree to help each other be joyful in all things.

Prayer: Dear Heavenly Father, show us how to have joy; show us how to be grateful for all the things we are able to do. Amen.

Notes

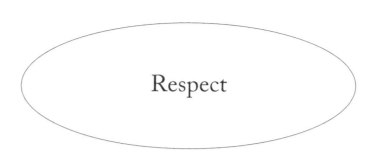

Respect

Respect everyone, and love your Christian brothers and sisters.

1 Peter 2:17 (NLT)

Everyone on this Earth desires respect, but not everyone deserves it. Respect is earned! You can't ask your mom and dad to respect you if you are doing nothing to show you deserve it. Mom, it's the same for a child to a parent; they don't just have to respect you because you are their parent. The Bible says right after "Children, honor your parents that fathers are not to anger their children.

Creating and holding respect is a journey, not a one-time event.

Below are a few guidelines that may help you on your journey to create mutual respect:

> **R**ights and responsibilities: We all have individual rights. If you were to research this in the Bible, you would find that the rights for parents are for them to expect their children to honor them. Children, too, have rights. The Bible says that if you raise them up in the way of the Lord, and they will walk in it. Along with all your rights come the responsibilities to perform them. That means you are held accountable to God for what you do or don't do.

Equality: We are all equal in God's sight. This means we are not to judge, nor are we to think we are greater than anyone else.

Standards of success and sensitivity: Success is not what the world says it is: having money and positioning. Success is how significant your life is. How have you touched others in a positive way or in a way that will bring them to a closer relationship with God?

Success is never success unless your relationships are above everything you do. Sensitivity to who others are and what their needs are will create significance in your life.

Power: Power is not ruling over; it is the ability to have God's power work through you to make what is wrong, right. With power comes courage to do what is right. Your source of power is God, not yourself.

Etiquette: Etiquette is rules of acceptable behavior. We must remember "acceptable behavior where we are at the time," as it varies from place to place. God's etiquette will speak above all human standards. What is that, you ask? – "Love one another at all costs!" With etiquette, you need to realize that there is always someone watching, especially little eyes. How you act will be duplicated by them.

Communication: The power of your tongue is life-giving or life-taking. Respectful communication means you work to build someone up, rather than tear them down. There are times when you need to stand your ground, but that doesn't mean at the expense of someone else's self-worth. The best way to communicate is through asking questions; try to understand their perception, walk a mile in their shoes (empathize).

Training and traditions: A mind that learns and grows in understanding is one of the greatest gifts God has given us. It means we never have to stay the same. We need to always be educating and growing our minds, opening it to new possibilities of how to do things or feel about things. Many of us are steeped in tradition, from our culture to our families, nationalities, or religions. God made us all differently; he doesn't want us to be all the same, but he does want us to accept each other as we are.

Talk Time

 Mother's Question: How have your words and actions been respectful or disrespectful? How do others show you respect?

 Daughter's Question: Same question as mom: How have your words and actions been respectful or disrespectful? How do others show you respect?

Agreement: We (your signatures) _____ and _____ agree to keep being respectful at the forefront of our thoughts and feelings, no matter what takes place.

Prayer: Dear Heavenly Father, the Bible says you are not a respecter of persons, which means your promises are for everyone, we are all the same in your sight; help us to remember that you ask us to see people as you do. Help us to remember that our actions and words towards others should be pleasing to you. Amen.

How You Feel is a Choice

Do not repay evil with evil or insult with insult,
but with blessing, because to this you were called
so that you may inherit a blessing.

1 Peter 3:9 (NIV)

One of the bigger life lessons I have learned is that happiness is a choice. I read a great book entitled just that. It was written by Doctors B. Minirth and Paul D. Meier. What it taught me most is that "I am in control of how I feel."

Before I continue with this discussion of today's topic, I want to stress that if you are suffering from chemical depression or an other mental illness, please make a choice to get help. If you continue to try to fight this on your own, the people around you will suffer as well as yourself.

There are many Christians who will tell you that if you can't overcome your depression, your problem is with your belief in Christ and what he can do and that it is not a medical issue. Please don't let that hinder you from finding help. If you broke your leg, would you not go to a doctor to have a cast put on? If you had diabetes, would you not take insulin? Chemical depression or other mental illnesses are real health conditions and need to be treated. God heals, and sometimes, he chooses to use medicine. Please don't hinder his ability.

Within healthy environments, we, women, are nurturers and are responsible for setting the tone in our homes, but just because we set a tone of peace does not mean everyone will follow suit and you will need to let people choose how they want to feel.

I, for a very long time, would let others' moods dictate how I felt. For example, if there was anger or an angry outburst, instead of choosing to react in a manner that would create a place where I could find peace, I would chose to walk on eggshells and try not to cause another outburst. Does this ring a bell for you? If it does, let me tell you, "No one makes you feel something." You choose to allow it.

I am perhaps older than you who are reading this, and it took me over forty years to get to the place of not allowing others or situations to control my feelings. If you can learn this now at your age, your life will have much more peace.

You won't be able to change your moods overnight; it will take a conscious effort to change your thought-life. But if you take the time to prayerfully ask God why situations make you feel the way you do and then ask him to show you how to change, he will. There are times when your prayers will need to be "Lord, if it is me who is wrong, please show me. If it is them, please change them." God is always the one who does the change, not you; it is best to let him do it, the results are far superior.

In a time of prayer, God spoke to me. He said that our thought-life, which controls how we feel, is a product of how you work to train your mind. He took me to the Bible where it talks about renewing our mind daily. He also said that through him, who strengthens us, we can do all things. He showed me that we can't do this on our own, it is impossible. But being able to cry out to him, saying "I can't do this, I don't want to feel like this anymore," and then throwing our hands up to him will open the door for him to help us make the change in how we feel.

He will also give us the grace to ask for forgiveness when what we have done has made others suffer because of our moods or actions.

Remember, we don't have to let situations (what is happening in our lives) or people make us feel bad, sad, or depressed. We have a choice Paul told us in Philippines 4:12 to be content in all things.

Talk Time

Mother's Question: When has someone else's mood dictated how you feel? When have your moods dictated how others feel?

Daughter's Question: Same question as Mom except perhaps thinking about a friend, sibling or maybe even your mom.

Agreement: We (your signatures) _____ and _____ agree to bring to each other's awareness (with love and grace) when our moods are affecting people negatively.

Prayer: Dear Heavenly Father, show us how to be happy and to keep our moods intact. Show us where there are areas of weakness that tend to bring us down, and then help us to change it. Amen.

Notes

The Gift of Doing for Others

There are different kinds of service, but we serve
the same Lord. God works in different ways, but
it is the same God who does the work in all of us.

1 Corinthians 12:5–6 (NLT)

Well, Mom, this topic, you may find, addresses something you deal with more. But, daughters, I bet if you think about it for a while, you can find areas that you too have to work at changing.

Do you ever hang on to tasks because no one can do it like you? The old adage, "If you want something done right, do it yourself."

So here it is: Daughters, have you done something your mom has asked you to do, only to find out she redid it right after you had completed the task? Okay, I am so guilty of this! I'll ask a family member or even an employee to do something, and if it is not done the way I would do it, I redo whatever it was. In my work and at home, I have been trying really hard to let that need to control and have it done my way, go and to let others do things their own way. I have started by first acknowledging that my way is not the only way to do things; I then go about finding out what other people are gifted at, and I allow them to do it and do it their way.

At our office, you can be guaranteed if I have to do any administrative tasks, it takes me three times longer, and you will find I make many mistakes. In fact writing this book, I have had to rely on many people to produce this product. But let me do a presentation, training session, or coaching, and I flourish, no help needed.

Life is so much easier if we work in our strengths and allow others to work in theirs. I know most of the things we like to delegate to others are because we don't like the tasks ourselves. This can lead us to believe that we shouldn't give those tasks to others because if we don't like it, they won't either. Usually, I find this untrue; people like or don't mind doing things I don't like to do.

What I believe is, if you allow others to do things for you, they will receive the blessings that can only come from serving others. Take on those tasks yourself and you may have stolen blessings from them. But if you will let them serve, especially where their gifts flourish, you have allowed them to do what God has created them for: to serve others.

One more note... there was a time that I felt if I let anyone do anything for me, I owed them something. I neglected to see the joy someone (family or friend) would have when I gave them an opportunity to bless me. If you allow them to give to you (keeping in mind your way is not the only way to have things done), you will in turn bless them.

Talk Time

 Mother's Question: Are you holding back from allowing others to help you?

 Daughter's Question: Are there times when Mom redoes what you have done? What is it, and how does that make you feel?

Agreement: We (your signatures) _____ and _____ agree to allow people to give to us. Remembering that our way is not the only way. Freeing them to experience working in the area God has gifted them in.

Prayer: Dear Heavenly Father, help us to see where you have gifted others and let us accept their gifts freely. Amen.

Notes

_____

_____

_____

_____

_____

_____

_____

_____

_____

_____

_____

_____

_____

_____

_____

_____

The Freedom God Has Given Us to Choose

> For if you live according to the sinful nature, you will die; but if by the Spirit you put to death the misdeeds of the body, you will live, because those who are led by the Spirit of God are sons of God.
>
> Romans 8:13–15 (NIV)

This is always a tough topic to get my head wrapped around, and I think it might be for you as well.

If God is really God, why doesn't he just stop us from making bad decisions? Or even tougher to get a handle on, why doesn't he stop people from doing bad things to others (why do bad things happen to good people)?

Here is what my finite mind can tell you: from the very beginning of time God gave his people the ability to choose. Adam and Eve chose to walk out of fellowship with him through such a simple thing as eating fruit that he asked them not to. It strikes me that they probably didn't even realize the extent of the consequences for that action; they were blinded by Satan. They didn't see into the future where they would no longer be able to have communion with God directly or that they would change things for all mankind. Why then did he let them be tempted? He wanted their hearts. He wanted them to love him and obey him because they wanted to, not because they had to.

Could you imagine what it would be like if we did only what God wanted us to do with no freedom to choose? We would be like puppets on a string, no need for emotions or intuitions. Actually, no need for a mind of our own! But in his generosity and love for us, he gave us free will and then he provides us his word and the teaching of it, so we would know right from wrong. He also gave us our conscience to lead us. His still small voice will direct us. If only we would listen.

With freedom of choice comes the freedom for us as humans to love our Creator. He is a gentleman and will never force his will or his love on us. He waits for us. Freedom of choice is a beautiful gift, but with all gifts, it is how we use them that will provide the reward.

Each of our journeys with God is completely unique; each of us will make our own choices and will live with the consequences or the blessings. Remember though, God is a God of restoration. Through his grace he can take our bad choices and turn them around for his glory and this devotional is one of his turn arounds. Glory be to God!

Talk Time

 Mother's Question: Discuss where you think God should have stepped in, and then pray for him to show you his wisdom for all your choices.

 Daughter's Question: Same as Mom: Discuss where you think God should have stepped in, and then pray for him to show you his wisdom for all your choices.

Agreement: We (your signatures) _____ and
_____ agree to keep each other accountable
to searching his word for help to make the right choices.

Prayer: Dear Heavenly Father, show us your wisdom.

> My prayer for you: May you hear God's still
> small voice and follow his direction, always.
> May your relationship as mother and daughter
> grow more intimate and be filled with grace and
> understanding.

—Love, Dawn

Notes

_____

_____

_____

_____

_____

_____

_____

_____

_____

_____

_____

_____

_____

_____

_____

Notes

_____

_____

_____

_____

_____

_____

_____

_____

_____

_____

_____

_____

_____

_____

_____

_____

_____

_____

_____

_____